Managed Equipment Services as a Conceptual Business Opportunity Model for the GCC with focus on UAE

An Institutional and Economic Analysis.

FSC
www.fsc.org
MIX
Papier aus verantwortungsvollen Quellen
Paper from responsible sources
FSC® C105338

Schriften zur Gesundheitsökonomie 21

Managed Equipment Services as a Conceptual Business Opportunity Model for the GCC with focus on UAE

An Institutional and Economic Analysis.

Michael J. Kloep

Michael J. Kloep
Hillesheim / Eifel
Friedrich-Alexander-Universität Erlangen – Nürnberg

Managed Equipment Services as a Conceptual Business Opportunity Model for the GCC with Focus on UAE - An Institutional and Economic Analysis.
Schriften zur Gesundheitsökonomie 21, HERZ, Burgdorf, 2012
Zugl. Erlangen, Nürnberg, Univ., Diss., 2011
Erstreferent: Professor Dr. Oliver Schöffski, Zweitreferent: Professor Dr. Harald Hungenberg
Promotionstermin: 23. November 2011
ISBN 978-3-936863-20-8

Herstellung: Books on Demand GmbH, Norderstedt

Table of Contents

List of Figures

List of Tables

List of Abbreviations

AED	**A**rab **E**mirates **D**irham
AG	**A**ktien**g**esellschaft (stock company)
BD	**B**ahraini **D**inar
BMI	**B**usiness **M**onitor **I**nternational
CAGR	**C**ontinuous **A**nnual **G**rowth **R**ate
CCASG	Gulf **C**ooperation **C**ouncil for the **A**rab **S**tates of the **G**ulf
CEO	**C**hief **E**xecutive **O**fficer
CIA	**C**entral **I**ntelligence **A**gency
CMMS	**C**ollege of **M**edicine and **M**edical **S**ciences
COGS	**C**ost **o**f **G**oods **S**old
COO	**C**hief **O**perating **O**fficer
CPQ	**C**entre for Healthcare **P**lanning and **Q**uality
CT	**C**omputed **T**omography
DBFO	**D**esign, **B**uild, **F**inance, **O**perate
DHA	**D**ubai **H**ealth **A**uthority
DHCC	**D**ubai **H**ealthcare **C**ity
DOHMS	Dubai **D**epartment **o**f **H**ealthcare and **M**edical **S**ervices
EBIT	**E**arnings **B**efore **I**nterest and **T**axes
EES	**E**ssential **E**quipment **S**ervice

EMRO	**E**astern **M**editerranean **R**egional Health System **O**bservatory
ENPC	**É**cole **n**ationale des **p**onts et **c**haussées
ENT	**E**ar, **N**ose, and **T**horax
EU	**E**uropean **U**nion
FDA	**F**ood and **D**rug **A**dministration
FDI	**F**oreign **D**irect **I**nvestment
FMHS	**F**aculty of **M**edicine and **H**ealth **S**ciences
GCC	**G**ulf **C**ooperation **C**ouncil
GDP	**G**ross **D**omestic **P**roduct
GE	**G**eneral **E**lectric
GNI	**G**ross **N**ational **I**ncome
HAAD	**H**ealth **A**uthority- **A**bu **D**habi
HC	**H**ealth**c**are
HMC	**H**amad **M**edical **C**ity
HTM	**H**ealth **T**echnology **M**anagement
IES	**I**ntermediate **E**quipment **S**ervice
IL	**I**nternational **L**iving
ISOs	**I**ndependent **S**ervice **O**rganizations
ISP	**I**ndependent **S**ervice **P**rovider
IT	**I**nformation **T**echnology
JCI	**J**oint **C**ommission **I**nternational
KPI	**K**ey **P**erformance **I**ndicators

KSA	**K**ingdom of **S**audi **A**rabia
ME	**M**iddle **E**ast
MES	**M**anaged **E**quipment **S**ervices
MoH	**M**inistry **o**f **H**ealth
MR	**M**agnetic **R**esonance
MRI	**M**agnetic **I**mage **R**esonance
NCB	**N**ational **C**ommercial **B**ank
NGDP	**N**on-Oil **G**ross **D**omestic **P**roduct
NHS	**N**ational **H**ealth **S**ervices
OEM	**O**riginal **E**quipment **M**anufacturer
OER	**O**il **E**xport **R**evenues
OMR	**Om**ani **R**iyal
OPEC	**O**rganization of **P**etroleum **E**xporting **C**ountries
PACS	**P**icture **A**rchiving and **C**ommunication **S**ystem
PCR	**P**olymerase **C**hain **R**eaction
PES	**P**remium **E**quipment **S**ervice
PET	**P**ositron **E**mission **T**omography
PFI	**P**rivate **F**inance **I**nitiative
POM	**P**ortfolio **O**wnership **M**atrix
PPP	**P**ublic **P**rivate **P**artnership
RF	**R**adiofrequency

RTA	**R**oads & **T**ransport **A**uthority
SAMA	**S**audi **A**rabian **M**onetary **A**gency
SEHA	**Se**rvices **H**ealth **A**bu Dhabi
SQU	**S**ultan **Q**aboos **U**niversity
SWOT	**S**trengths, **W**eaknesses, **O**pportunities, and **T**hreats
TEI	**T**otal **E**conomic **I**mpact
UAE	**U**nited **A**rab **E**mirates
UHL	**U**niversity **H**ospital of **L**eicester
UK	**U**nited **K**ingdom
UN	**U**nited **N**ations
UNICEF	**U**nited **N**ations **I**nternational **C**hildren's **E**mergency **F**und
US	**U**nited **S**tates
USA	**U**nited **S**tates of **A**merica
VIP	**V**ery **I**mportant **P**erson
WAM	**W**akalat **A**nba'a al-E**m**arat
WHO	**W**orld **H**ealth **O**rganization
WHOSIS	**W**orld **H**ealth **O**rganisation **S**tatistical **I**nformation **S**ystem

1. Introduction

1.1 Purpose of the Study

The purpose of this dissertation is to determine the success potential for Managed Equipment Services in the Gulf Cooperation Council (GCC) states and its ability to increase the quality and availability of healthcare, as well as cost and time efficiencies, particularly in the management and maintenance of radiology equipment. This dissertation focuses on the UAE in general and Abu Dhabi in particular. The concentration on the latter is due to differences between the healthcare industry of each Emirate. As the capital of UAE, Abu Dhabi has the best healthcare industry for evaluation due to its strong economic performance and representative demographics. Abu Dhabi is the wealthiest Emirate in the UAE and is also often referred to as "the world's richest city" (Tatchell, 2009). Healthcare equipment and services in Abu Dhabi is one of the sectors that are expected to drive economic growth. The Emirate was therefore chosen as an initial market for launching an MES program. Conceptual models that could be used to verify the feasibility of MES were developed. Following, these models could be adapted to the GCC region and especially, to UAE.

1.2 Scope of the Study

The scope of this dissertation is limited to evaluating the potential of GCC states' medical equipment and services market for running an independent Managed Equipment Services (MES) program. In this case, the focus is largely placed on cutting edge medical imaging equipment in the field of radiology.

In general, the analysis and the relevant information provided are taken from the point of the view of the government with regards to the factors required to advance the healthcare sector. This view however can be adapted to fit other entities in the healthcare sector since the healthcare provider, payer, OEM, and the independent MES provider's goals are often directly linked to governmental goals and targets (e.g. to increase the quality of care while decreasing the time and cost of treatment).

As such, an overview of the GCC states' healthcare industry (with a special focus on the equipment and services markets) is provided. The emirate of Abu Dhabi however, is taken as an ideal model due to its strong healthcare infrastructure, financing capabilities, and healthcare system challenges that could be strengthened with an MES program. A detailed analysis of the Emirate's healthcare market is therefore provided. Since most MES programs are currently run by OEMs that specialize in radiology equipment and services, the dissertation has emphasized the potential of an MES program for radiology units in Abu Dhabi. MES as a business opportunity for OEMs was therefore also evaluated through a well used industry assessment tool.

The selected elements and aspects in this dissertation are theoretical and generic. As such they need to be adapted and modified for a business case and plan based on the given environment. The development and chosen theoretical scenarios and paradigms are based on the local environment and feedback from healthcare professionals. Prof. Dr. Oliver Schöffski, director of Health Management at the University of Erlangen-Nürnberg and a health economics specialist, indicates that economic efficiency health is the umbrella term for all studies in the healthcare sector where medical measures are economically evaluated. Prof. Schöffski points out that most of these studies are done for the pharmaceutical industry. The databases for non pharmaceutical studies are considerably poorer (Schöffski & Schulenburg, 2008). Based on the research conducted, this statement is especially valid for the GCC region. An additional challenge is that published surveys and research reports are not created on an annual or consistent basis. Therefore, the latest data on a specific topic was provided. Nevertheless, the information and data gained through primary research methods validate the existing information collected from published sources. Thus an indication of the current situation of the GCC healthcare market and its projected direction of growth has been reviewed, analyzed and validated. Accordingly, an approach towards increasing the quality and the delivery of healthcare services has been developed. The status of health and healthcare delivery created the demand for medical equipment. Trends and opportunities in the healthcare industry in this region as well as its status are evaluated because radiology equipment and services as a market within the healthcare industry is directly linked and thereby affected by overall trends, opportunities and status of the healthcare industry.

1.3 Structure and Approach of the Study

Through the process of validating this thesis, conceptual models for Managed Equipment Services structured as a business opportunity for the Gulf Cooperation Council were developed. The purpose as previously stated is to investigate whether an MES approach would raise the welfare of healthcare by increasing the quality of care while simultaneously decreasing the cost of care in the GCC countries using data on United Arab Emirates and Abu Dhabi as validation.

The dissertation is divided in to seven sections. The fist section provides an overview of medical equipment, in general, and the equipment associated with the different fields of radiology, in particular. The second section focuses on MES. In this section, MES is defined and the services that are offered through an MES program are covered in depth. Furthermore, the benefits, of MES have been evaluated for each of the direct stakeholders identified (Payers, OEMs, healthcare providers). The risks absorbed by the MES and healthcare providers are also assessed. Accordingly, a SWOT analysis was conducted.

Based on the data and information in the previous section, the third section presents the conceptual service, ownership, pricing, and stakeholder models have been developed from a global perspective taking into account the regional realities in the second section. In the fourth section, an overview of the GCC region is presented by introducing each country and providing information on the economic standing and healthcare industry of each country. In the fifth section, MES as a business opportunity in the GCC is evaluated by identifying areas of opportunity in the GCC healthcare industry and through a theoretical analysis using Porter's Five Forces. The sixth section focuses on UAE and especially Abu Dhabi. In this section the healthcare infrastructure of UAE is described followed by an assessment of the equipment management, maintenance and procurement practices using information from the survey conducted as well as from interviews and secondary research. The healthcare industry is described with a specific orientation towards radiology.

Based on the data provided, recommendations for implementing MES in GCC region were formulated in the last section followed by an outlook on the future of healthcare in GCC. This paper on hand was thus concluded with a summary of the main findings.

2. Managed Equipment Services (MES)

This chapter defines and discusses the different elements and essentials associated with Managed Equipment Service. After the theoretical definition of the equipment and service portfolio, options are described and discussed including the benefits, risks and examples of existing global MES projects and providers that provide insights into the structure and approach of such a scheme.

2.1 Medical Equipment

Based on the defined scope of this thesis, the focus is mainly on large and medical imaging equipment in the field of radiology. The terms used for such equipment is medical device or medical / healthcare- equipment.

The challenges posed by the complexity of the long lifetime large equipment cost and the required knowledge and experience to purchase and maintain such equipment effectively and efficiently are the reasons for this focus (Hanna, 2001).

2.1.1 Medical Equipment Innovation & Outlook

Medical Equipment innovation is making a great contribution to the health and quality of life by extending the ability of physicians to diagnose and treat diseases. Medical devices improve the quality of life and save lives on the therapeutic side. Safer operations, significant shorter hospital stays, less pain and trauma can be realized with invasive technologies.

The mainstream practice of medicine has significantly changed with the considerable attention of technologies such as computer-assisted tomography and magnetic resonance imaging. Diagnostic technology includes capital equipment imagers' analytical techniques using high-resolution chromatography, polymerase chain reaction (PCR), and monoclonal antibodies. These technologies provide physicians with new, accurate, and rapid information. Medical devices often require the contribution of a diverse array of scientific and engineering expertise.

Innovation and development of such equipment extend well beyond laboratories; in many instances, clinicians are discovering new indications and breakthroughs.

Innovation requires insight, time, sustainable financial resources, and often luck. One example for the financial need is the cost-intensive payments to regulations for new technology. As such, developing and implementing new medical equipment is far beyond just producing the 'latest widget'. (Hanna, 2001)

The medical device market has a great future potential and could be the next candidate for an outburst business like what happened in the past to Information Technology (Schmitt-Rüth, Esslinger, & Schöffski, 2007).

2.1.2 Medical Equipment Quality and Regulation

In the context of the design and development of medical devices quality supports safety and performance. Safety and performance should enhance durability and in turn durability should enable flexibility. Flexibility consequently should facilitate speed. Speed correlates to costs. Evolution of quality proved a preponderance of focus on manufacturing medical device parts. (El-Haik & Mekki, 2008) Based on this fact, the guidelines and regulations for OEM are increasing dramatically. The Food and Drug Administration (FDA) is the main medical equipment regulator in the Unites States of America, and also one of the main regulators worldwide. The FDA Center for Devices and Radiological Health takes important measures to streamline regulatory processes. However the market implementation of new medical devices is a complex process (Hanna, 2001).

To ensure the guidelines and regulations, quality management programs are implemented. Such programs monitor treatment type and duration, for example the outpatient services (Berger, 2008).

2.1.3 Medical Equipment Manufacturer

The original equipment manufacturer of medical equipment is a business entity that produces complex equipment (such as medical equipment) from components usually bought from other manufacturers and sells the equipment under its own brand name either directly, or through an independent vendor (Encyclopædia Britannica, 2011).

The OEM, as described in the *Medical Equipment Innovation & Outlook* as well as in the *Medical Equipment Quality and Regulation* sections has to abide by many standards and principles; such as quality and regulatory guidelines and specifications, has proven to be very challenging. Large equipment manufacturers by virtue of their size and resources are typically better equipped to abide by these regulations. This is the reason why mainly large equipment manufacturers can be found in the selected equipment market. In the same manner, one can find some smaller equipment vendors for some niche products. However this is very rare due to the high cost of implementation of new medical equipment. Nerveless the potential is huge due to the extreme technology movement and development in the medical equipment market (Hanna, 2001).

With different medical equipment manufacturers, the pricing model of medical equipment often can go down below the cost of production. Therefore the needed margin has to be made with a long-term service contract. Equipment services for life-cycle intensive equipment are more profitable than the sale of the equipment. Often, to be able to offer such a service, a high quality service network needs to be established on a worldwide basis. While this is costly; on the other hand, the medical providers are willing to pay high margin for high quality service (Litteral & Altay, 2011). Service quality is one of the main important selling points for patients and therefore also for healthcare providers. Delivering quality healthcare depends on using quality products (medical equipment) and services. (Duggirala, Rajendran, & Anantharaman, 2008) The healthcare providers observe that complex and cutting edge medical technology is practical only when it is actually working and can be used on a daily business case. However, they often understand that high technology needs high maintenance. (Healthcare Provider 1, 2011)

For instance, the possibility of a software upgrade is higher on new software as it is on more established software. Nevertheless, upstanding market approvals and quality regulations are extremely complex and comprehensive for high technology equipment. This again develops the need for complex and wide-ranged service and maintenance. (Singh & Shi, 2008)

The OEM optimizes the possibilities for surpassing high quality service as much as possible. For instance, providing a remote service (being able to connect online to a machine to update software concerns) and covering the world with certain service headquarters (for example for spare parts), could facilitate faster maintenance for their medical equipment all over the world.

This set-up turned out to be very complex and costly for the OEMs. An additional factor for this is also that the service business is normally not the core business of a manufacturer. (Ben-Daya, Duffuaa, Raouf, Knezevic, & Ait-Kadi, 2009)

2.1.4 Medical Equipment Cost of Ownership and life-cycle cost

The cost of ownership includes direct and indirect expenses of medical devices over its lifetime. Typically, the expenses include the initial cost for the equipment, including installation and initial training costs and its long-term expenses. Such long-term expenses include equipment service, upgrades, ongoing training, supplies, connectivity and upgrades. However, healthcare providers have recently begun to include an account of the full range of cost-of-ownership factors in their acquisition process and technology assessment. This calculation includes the costs for acquisition, as well as operating and maintenance costs like installation, supplies, downtime, training, spare parts, test equipment and tools and downtime[1]. (David & Judd, 2000) Maintenance must be carried out regardless of expenditures, as maintenance plays an important role towards achieving production targets. The success and effectiveness of maintenance depends on the effort and care put into estimating its cost accurately. (Mishra, 2006)

Based on estimates, the actual purchase price makes only 20% of the total life-cycle cost of ownership. Therefore, the typical product life-cycle costs include the initial purchase price, shipping, renovation, installation, supplies, associated disposables, cost per use, and similar quantitative measures. In addition, the life-cycle cost can take into account the costs for staff training, ease of use, service, and many other cost factors. (David & Judd, 2000) Other than life-cycle costing,

1 The time when the medical device cannot be used because of ongoing maintenance services. (OEM Service Manger, 2011)

there are also other methods of equipment costing such as value functions and performance auditing (Mishra, 2006).

2.2 Radiology

Radiology services encompasses all specialties that use ionizing and in some cases non-ionizing radiation to view and treat internal anatomy. Radiology has been used since 1895 when William Roentgen first discovered the x-ray. The use of radiation is continuously increasing, and technological advances have allowed for more provision of more precise and timely treatments for patients suffering from debilitating diseases. (Muellner, et al., 2009) The three main branches of Radiology are classified according to the manner the techniques are used: diagnostic radiology, therapeutic radiology, interventional radiology (Lopiano & Del Fava, 2008) (Griffin, 2010).

2.2.1 Diagnostic Radiology

Diagnostic imaging is used to uncover, diagnose, and examine patient ailments. There are five main diagnostic imaging techniques used: radiography, fluoroscopy, computed tomography, magnetic resonance imaging and ultrasound (A.D.A.M. Incorporated, 2011).

- **Radiography:** Radiography or the use of x-rays is the first imaging technique to be introduced to medicine. X-rays produce a two dimensional black and white image (radiograph) of the body. X-rays are used to detect bone fractures, discover object foreign in the body, and examine internal anatomy. (U.S. Food and Drug Administration , 2011)
- **Fluoroscopy:** Fluoroscopy is a technique that is very similar to radiography; a fluoroscopy device emits a continuous stream of X-rays to allow technicians to visualize the anatomy while the device operates. Fluoroscopy allows medical professionals to view and detect abnormalities in functioning organs as well as assist in a range of procedures such as the placement of pacemakers. (Lusted, 2008)

- **Computed tomography (CT):** A computed tomography (CT) scanner provides a three-dimensional view of the anatomy by emitting multiple x-rays from a variety of angles. This allows physicians to view images that have a much higher level of clarity than the images produced through radiography. CT scans are commonly used to view the abdomen, chest, and pelvis. Computed tomography devices emit high levels of ionized radiation and thus safety procedures must be followed carefully. (Lopiano & Del Fava, 2008)
- **Magnetic Image Resonance (MRI):** Unlike other imaging techniques, MRIs produce images using a powerful magnet that interacts with different molecules in the body. As do CTs, MRIs produce three dimensional images; the images generated by an MRI provide for a much higher level of contrast between soft tissues in the body. An MRI therefore is considered by medical professionals as the ideal tool to be used when attempting to reveal underlying physiologic and metabolic processes. (Griffin, 2010)
- **Ultrasound:** Ultrasound imaging (also known as sonography) uses high frequency sound waves that penetrate the skin and strike specific tissues; echoes are produced which are then electronically converted into an anatomic image that is displayed on a video screen. Ultrasound imaging is commonly used in obstetrics to detect problems in other internal structures, such as the gallbladder, kidney, and heart. (Lopiano & Del Fava, 2008)

2.2.2 Interventional Radiology

Interventional radiology as defined by the Society of Interventional Radiology and Cardiovascular and Interventional Radiological Society of Europe and Springer Science is both a therapeutic and diagnostic specialty that consists of a broad range of minimally invasive image guided therapeutic procedures as well as invasive diagnostic imaging. Interventional radiology is primarily used for diseases and elements related to the vascular, gastrointestinal, hepatobiliary, genitourinary, pulmonary, musculoskeletal, and, in some countries, the central nervous system. Interventional radiology is considered as an integral part of medical care. (Journal of Vascular Interventional Radiology, 2010) Interventional radiology treats diseases non-surgically through employing a combination of the medial imaging (from x-rays to MRIs) in conjunction with various catheter and injection techniques to treat a disease (E Lakhan, Kaplan, Laird, & Leiter, 2009). The most common IR procedure used is an angiography, which is used to treat blocked or narrowed arteries. In an angiography, a catheter is inserted through the artery to the narrowed segment where a balloon at the tip of the catheter is inflated and then deflated allowing the blockage to pass. A combined laser–catheter procedure is also used to treat blocked arteries. (Lopiano & Del Fava, 2008)

2.2.3 Therapeutic Radiology

Therapeutic radiology (also known as radiation therapy) is used to treat disease with high doses of ionizing radiation. Therapeutic radiation is predominantly used to treat cancer (radiation oncology) and cancer related diseases. Radiation therapy delivers high doses of radiation to the body part affected with cancer and prevents cancerous cells from multiplying while simultaneously preserves the surrounding tissue as much as possible. Radiation therapy is administered over multiple sessions that last over several weeks allowing healthy tissue that was exposed to radiation the time required to heal. (Lusted, 2008)

2.3 Definition of MES

Consequently, the term Managed Equipment Services has three facets/ words in it: 'Management ('managed')', 'Equipment', and 'Service'.

Management ('Managed') is defined as, "Working with and through other people to accomplish the objectives of both the organization and its members" (Montana & Charnov, 2000, p. 1). Management activities include planning, organizing, staffing, leading, and controlling; getting results effectively through other people by the process of delegation. Based on this quote, Management is a combination of executing different activities through resources to accomplish objectives. (Montana & Charnov, 2000)

Equipment is defined as: "A set of tools, devices, or kit assembled for a specific purpose" (Collins English Dictionary, 2011). The root of the word equipment; 'equip' means to supply with necessary materials (Collins English Dictionary, 2011). Service is defined in this context of active service as "an act of helpful activity, help, or aid" or in the entered service view as "employment as a servant" (Collins English Dictionary, 2011, p. 1). The existing definitions show that service is seen as a combination of the terms. When the terms are combined then this could mean executing different activities thought physical or people or things to accomplish and contribute a serving objective.

Managed Equipment Services is applied in other sectors as well, however, within the scope of this study MES is defined and applied to the healthcare sector. This again limits the scope of the definition. There are a number of different definitions. The following ones are the most common.

The definitions provided are based on an MES relationship between Medical OEMs and healthcare providers and healthcare MES provider, as well as other 3rd parties.

Managed Equipment Services essentially ensure a long-term sustainable investment in healthcare technology and guarantees and delivers timely financial benefits (General Electric Company, 2011). Even if the term "Managed Equipment Services" is also used in other business sectors it has a connection to the healthcare sector. MES is a new model of partnership with a private sector medical equipment provider that usually lasts for a period of fifteen years through which the MES provider manages all equipment related responsibilities including ongoing replacement and disposal of medical equipment (Siemens AG, 2011).

Through MES, the knowledge and experience of purchasing, installing, user trainings, asset management, reporting, managing and maintaining of a medical equipment portfolio is outsourced by a healthcare provider like a Hospital or Clinic. This allows medical practitioners to focus on their core business; providing patients with the famous Taguchi standards quality of healthcare while having access to maintained equipment based on the agreed terms. (Balakrishnan, 1999) Healthcare provider also benefit from a clearer and predictable cost structure

(Asteral, 2011). The term Managed Equipment Services is consequently compromised of three facets/ words; Management ('Managed')', 'Equipment', and 'Service'. MES is also consistently associated with outsourcing. Hence the definition of MES is a combination of these three words. Activities are outsourced if other party can perform the outsourced work process/ activity more effectively and efficiently for the healthcare provider. Activities are also outsourced if other more important responsibilities have a higher demand for the healthcare provider's resources. As such, in order to outsource an activity, the other party (MES provider in this case) should have the ability to perform more efficiently and effectively than the healthcare provider. (Power, Desouza, & Bonifazi, 2006)

Based on both the primary research and secondary research conducted for this analysis, the definitions and services offered are not clearly defined and tend to vary from one OEM/ MES provider to another. The following approach and design has been taken from the view of an independent MES provider.

2.4 MES Services and Portfolio

Managed Equipment Services provides a one-stop turnkey solution for the equipment that is under the MES contract. Through an MES program, the healthcare provider would have a single point of contact for the comprehensive solutions agreed upon in the contract. Thus, the MES provider would independently undertake full responsibility for performing and integrating the outsourced activities within the framework of the healthcare providers operations. (Asteral, 2011)

Measurable, transparent, and clear 'Key Performance Indicators' will be defined through assessing the healthcare provider's existent of performance for the services that are to be outsourced. Accordingly, the tasks related to these services are optimized and performed in a more efficient and effective manner (Parmenter, 2010). Monitoring is a vital factor that enables continuous improvement through which performance targets are achieved (Loper, 1993). Both parties have an equal stake and thus interest in meeting defined targets (i.e. The MES provider wants avoid penalties incurred when performance indicators are not met, and the healthcare provider wants maximum operational efficiency). As such they will both work to continuously optimize and improve their joint performance. (MES Provider 2, 2010)

Typically the MES provider is either an independent service provider that has contracts with OEMs or an OEM that provides either all or an agreed-upon percentage of its own equipment to the trust. MES has lead to an increase in productivity by ensuring that medical professionals constantly have access to high quality equipment and by substantially decreasing equipment downtime. Patient waiting time is thus reduced, leading to higher patient turnover, and a reduction in cost per patient. Based on the urgency and level of resource the procurement of an MES implementation takes 6-12 month. (Asteral, 2011) The next figure illustrates the management cycle for hospital equipment. The services provided by an MES provider cover most of the tasks outline in the diagram: asset management planning, establishment of new equipment needs and priorities, identification of procurement options and allocation of resources, the assessment of utilization and replacement needs, equipment disposal, and equipment maintenance. Next, the services offered by an MES provider are described. (Pathology In Practice, 2007)

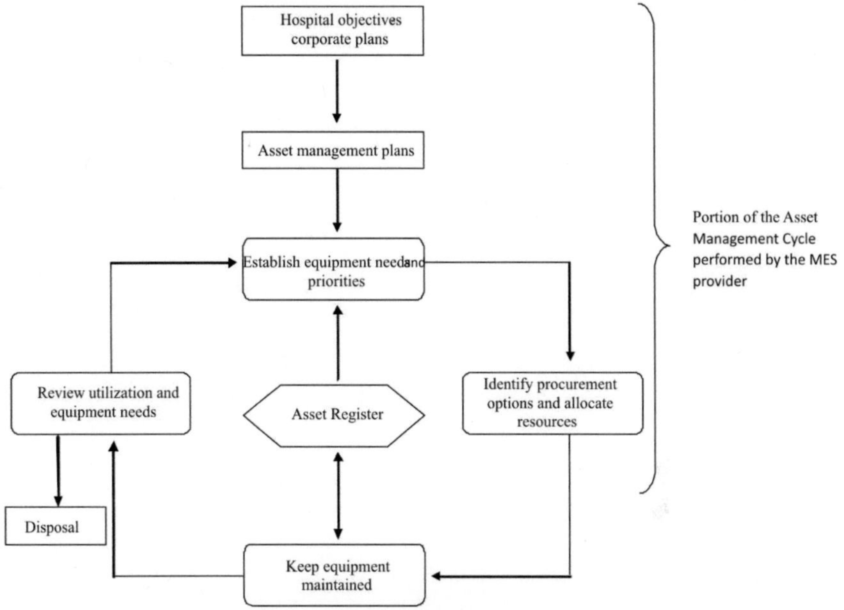

Figure 1: Asset Management Cycle (Cameron, 2003)

Based on an analysis of the interviews carried out with MES experts and healthcare professionals, as well as the results of the survey conducted, the services offered under an MES program have been identified and defined. This service paradigm shows a wheel with the possible service options selected. These elements represent a range of the portfolio and therefore the points of cooperation, an MES provider would offer to the healthcare provider. Or on the other hand, the responsibilities of a healthcare provider could be passed or outsourced to an MES provider.

The main framework and elements are long term strategic alliance (including defining the performance framework, targets and future alignment), Equipment Planning (inclusive of an agreed long term investment plan, equipment rationalisation and infrastructure design), Finance, Procurement & implementation, User Training, Insurance, Asset Management, Performance & Safety monitoring, Maintenance (including providing a hotline/ standby services) and Technology

Adjustment. The Service Wheel in the next figure illustrates the services identified.

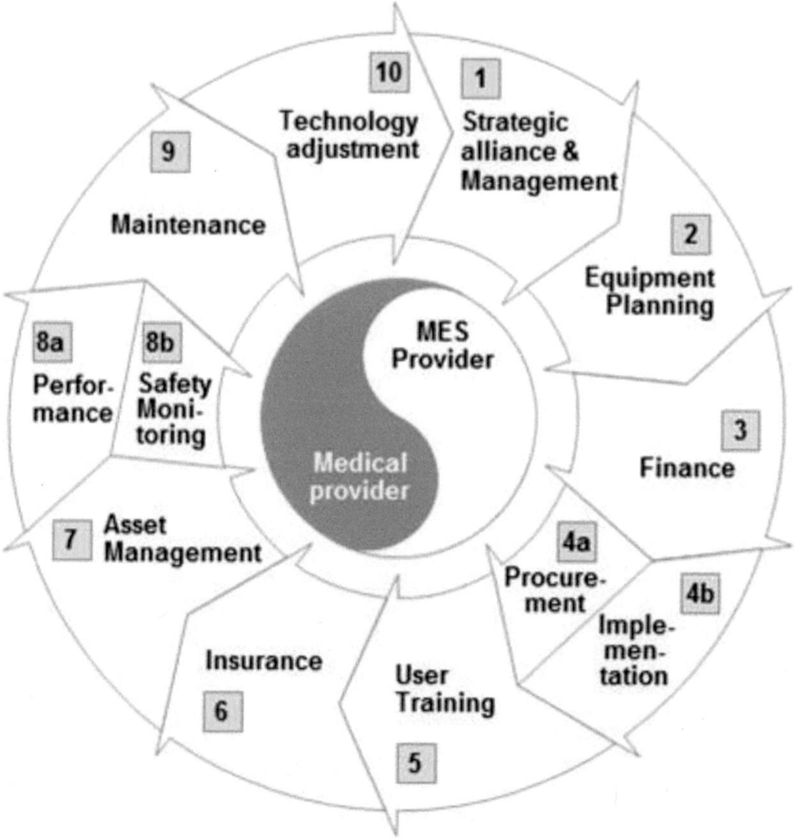

Figure 2: MES Service Wheel[2]

The services reflect the main points of the collaboration between the MES provider and the healthcare provider. The independence through which the MES provid-

[2] The Service Wheel has been designed based on an analysis of the secondary research collected.

er operates and the synergies created are the unique selling points of the elements provided on the Service Wheel. Each element of the service wheel has thus been described. Within the scope of this paper, the MES provider does not operate the equipment and thus related costs and risks have not been incorporated in the description of these services. This is the main factor that differentiates MES from the traditional outsourcing frameworks.

2.4.1 Strategic Alliance & Management

Strategic Alliance Management is a vital factor for managing the business relationship between two partners; this is due to the dramatic rise in the importance of strategic management within the academic and the practical business world. Businesses are increasingly driven towards strategy analysis, strategy definition and strategy implementation (Hungenberg & Wulf, 2005). As such, strategic alliance within an MES program has been designated as the starting and ultimate point of an MES program. Since the average length of an MES Contact is 15-30 years, the long term goals, strategies, and objectives need to be aligned with implementation between the cooperating parties. This should include both the performance framework and the targets. (Asteral, 2011)

Prof. Dr. Harald Hungenberg who holds the Chair for Strategic Management at the University Erlangen-Nürnberg and is the affiliated professor at the School of International Management at ENPC in Paris, points out, that different studies proved over and over again that the actual transfer of the strategy is more important than the type of the strategy. Therefore, ensuring the transfer of the strategy is an essential element (Hungenberg, 2003). In addition Prof. Hungenberg points out that to be able to effectively understand progression and the most efficient business approach, it is essential to question the business target. A business target is typically defined as a desired, future state. (Hungenberg & Wulf, 2004) Such mentioned strategy definition and transfer need to be ensured by the stakeholders. This strategic alliance should therefore include the planned offerings, intensive knowledge and expertise exchange of the products, distribution channels, technology transfer, procurement capability, and project funding/ capital, and equipment on a short and long-term basis. Through cooperating and collaborating with multiple parties, a synergy is formed that provides additional benefits that each stakeholder would not have been able to attain independently. Synergy effects are optimized through the process of technology transfer and knowledge/ expertise sharing which occurs in an MES program (Mowery, Oxley, & Silverman, 1996).

Healthcare providers are always faced with burgeoning costs that are difficult to contain; proper equipment management through an MES program ensures cost effective performance (World Health Organization, 2006). The Strategic Alliance and Management element of the Service Wheel should to cover all the management related fundamentals within an outsourcing relationship of a project. The following elements are concurrent with observations made by healthcare providers (Healthcare Provider 1, 2011) (Healthcare Provider 2, 2011):

- **Work Administration**
  This critical task ensures that the work that has been undertaken is effectively and efficiently completed. Contract management and the initial assessment of the project plan is part of this task. Tracking work assignments, deliverables and resource consumption, and project timeline alignment is also included. (Power, Desouza, & Bonifazi, 2006)
- **Communication Management**
  Ensuring effective and transparent communication between the healthcare provider and the MES provider (Power, Desouza, & Bonifazi, 2006).
- **Knowledge Management**
  A continuous, transparent, and effective exchange of new knowledge and experience that must occur (Power, Desouza, & Bonifazi, 2006).
- **Personnel Management**
  In addition to typical resource planning, this task is also needed to ensure that the healthcare provider and the MES provider resources can and will work with that of the other stakeholders. These stakeholders however must have clearly separate roles and responsibilities. (Power, Desouza, & Bonifazi, 2006)

- **Financial Management**
  This task should clarify and periodically asses the budget and framework of the contract based on the payment scheme (Power, Desouza, & Bonifazi, 2006).

2.4.2 Equipment Planning

Equipment planning typically starts with defining and identifying the healthcare provider's equipment requirements, as well as the standard of the equipment's performance throughout its lifetime.

A. Equipment Rationalization

Prior to the commencement of the contract, the MES provider conducts an audit of existing assets, a workflow analysis and a technology assessment. The decision based on which equipment will be purchased occurs through a process of rationalization and standardization. Using the information gained from these processes and from the provider's expertise, the MES provider provides efficient and cost effective equipment management solution. The MES provider takes over the risk of equipment replacement. In order to ensure that the facility does not bear any extra costs due to equipment replacement, each piece of equipment is evaluated by placing it in a band that identifies where it sits in the spectrum of technology currently available for that type of equipment. Typically there are four bands that range from high-tech equipment to basic work-horse equipment. When a piece of equipment is due for replacement, the new piece is selected from the range of equipment that is available in the same band; thus removing the hospital from the risk of product replacement. While the band of the equipment and type of equipment that will be provided is sealed in the investment plan outlined in the MES, contract, the plan is meant to be flexible, and can easily be altered by amending the contract. (Asteral, 2011)

B. New Equipment Selection Consultation

Before selecting a new piece of equipment, the equipment database, which is also managed by the MES provider, is audited. The MES provider then informs the medical provider/ cooperation partner of the equipment that should be transferred back to the provider and the cost of this process. If agreed upon, the MES provider will handle the process of equipment replacement and disposal in a manner that should is designed to minimise disruption. In some cases, the MES provider is responsible for medical equipment disposal. (Asteral, 2011)

This offers additional opportunity for an MES approach by offering or selling used equipment.[3] Since the MES provider has a large number of customers (other healthcare providers), and thereby bargaining power, the MES provider is able to sell the medical equipment to a wider range of buyers. Depending on the ownership of the equipment, the MES provider could pull out or buy back the old equipment from one customer (such as a research university hospital) that has advanced technology requirements. The MES provider could then refurbish the equipment and sell it to another customer that has lower technology requirements. (Asteral, 2011)

2.4.3 Finance

Due to the increasing cost of healthcare in the GCC countries, there is a need for cost-effective financial decisions to be made by an entity that has both the technological and financial expertise. (Alpen Capital Limited, 2009) According to Healthcare Financial Management Association, healthcare financial executives who are often given tight budgets find it very difficult to make decisions regarding the evaluation, acquisition, financing, and disposal of medical equipment (Conbeer, 2007). The main challenges that these financial executives face are:

- Finding the reliable, objective sources of technical information required (Conbeer, 2007)
- Choosing the right financing vehicle that best fits within the requirement (Conbeer, 2007)
- Being able to ensure a suitable long-term integration plan for the equipment, as well as maintenance/ up-keeping of the healthcare equipment (Conbeer, 2007)

3 Also called refurbished equipment. (OEM Service Manger, 2011)

MES providers devise tailored investment plans that cover the entire length of the contract. Upon the commencement of the contract, the MES provider obtains the necessary capital funding for the medical facility either by using the entity's own financial resources or through bank loans. (Asteral, 2011) As a result the capital requirement is written off the trust's balance sheet. Bank loans also ensure that the MES provider has the necessary funding prior to signing the contract. In order to secure such a large loan, the MES provider must have a track record with a number of financial institutions, and as such can obtain competitive interest rates. The medical facility thus benefits by paying a fixed fee taken from the medical facility's revenue budget. As a result the facility avoids the added costs of inflation, as well as continuously increasing equipment and maintenance costs. (Pathology In Practice, 2007)

2.4.4 Procurement & Implementation

A. Procurement

Several thousand manufacturers worldwide produce a multitude of healthcare equipment. Selecting, procuring, and implementing the right medical devices is a very complex procedure that requires extensive experience and knowledge. Additionally, choosing equipment that does not improve either individual or public health normally leads to either inappropriately using the equipment or not using the equipment altogether. (Smith & Correa, 2005) If this occurs financial resources are wasted. In general, there are several barriers to choosing medical devices; the main barrier is that many lack the ability to rationally and objectively choose equipment without regard to personal fascination with technology and for cutting-edge devices, marketing misconceptions, high running costs and incorrect information about the medical device. Often, medical devices are chosen without carrying out objective evaluation of information; this could cause the healthcare provider to incur many hidden costs. (World Health Organization, 2010) Continuously escalating costs constitutes another challenge; healthcare providers find it very difficult control their expenses. Proper equipment management however, ensures cost effective performance. (World Health Organization, 2006)

B. Implementation

Typically the OEM is in charge of installing all of the equipment that has been procured by the healthcare provider. (Nah & Osifo-Dawodu, 2007) Installation is generally a lengthy process that involves pre-testing the equipment before it is shipped to the healthcare provider, then testing it after it has been delivered and then again after it has been installed, in order to test that it is functioning properly. Generally inspection certificates (from the healthcare provider) need to be obtained for each testing phase. If the equipment is under the service contract, the MES provider takes-up a supervisory role over the installation process to ensure its success. The MES provider supervises the process to make sure that the user interface of new equipment is compatible with that of the existing equipment.

The installation process requires strong coordination between the equipment supplier (OEM) the customs clearing agent, and sometimes the trainer (Nah & Osifo-Dawodu, 2007). In this case the MES provider is added to this list but takes a rather supervisory role and manages the coordination with these entities to control the standards and the interfaces used. For example, hospitals installing Picture Archiving and Communications System (PACs); a communication and archiving systems used for viewing and archiving radiographic images. For a PACs system to work, it must be compatible with the radiographic imaging devices in the healthcare facility; the MES provider in this case makes sure that devices installed are compatible with the PACs system in place. (Keller, 2004)

The MES provider also makes sure that the equipment is installed in line with the safety standards required. Western regulatory bodies such as the Food and Drug Administration (FDA) in USA, and the United Kingdom Medicines and Healthcare Products Regulatory Agency in the UK have a high impact on the GCC healthcare market. According to interviews conducted with healthcare providers, due to the lack of comprehensive regulation and the number of international healthcare operators in the GCC countries, healthcare providers adopt the standards mandated by international regulatory bodies as their own. One example is the U.S. Food and Drug Administration (FDA). (Healthcare Provider 1, 2011)

The scope of the FDA's authority is generally restricted to market approval information, safety and performance efficiency (World Health Organization, 2010).

In some cases, the medical facility will take up an MES program at the same time as a rebuilding or renovation program. The MES provider can then communicate with the architect to ensure that the design of the building or room meets the current and future requirements of the equipment that will be used in the hospital. Incorporating this service in an MES contract ensures that the hospital infrastructure will have the capacity to operate continuously advanced medical equipment. This ensures the feasibility of implementing equipment upgrades without requiring the medical facility to make further investments in building maintenance and restructuring. This service thus leads to a decrease in the facility's long-term infrastructure expenses. (Asteral, 2011)

Based on the points factors assessed, the MES provider will therefore have a rational view in consideration of the needs. Additionally, the provider supplies the needed colloquialism based on his industrial experience and knowledge from other healthcare provider (Sallas, Lane, Mathews, Watkins, & Wiley-Patton, 2007).

2.4.5 User Training

The incidence for errors in regards to equipment use is very high, most of which are attributed to lack of sufficient training (World Health Organization, 2010). The literature shows that the leading cause of hospitalized patients' death is medical equipment errors (Tavakoli, Karami, Rezai, Esfandiari, & Khashayar, 2007). The MES provider is responsible for training the responsible staff members on the proper usage of equipment and other related processes required for specific hospital functions (Asteral, 2011). Training is done to ensure that the necessary working procedures across the hospital are standardized and performed accurately (Nah & Osifo-Dawodu, 2007). Such training results in reductions in procedure time, thereby reducing the probability of patient inconvenience. Not to mention, improper training programs may cause a number of patient-filed lawsuits against hospitals (Cowan, 2000). Training sessions are done upon the commencement of the MES contract, and then can be done on a routine basis to ensure that procedures are conducted correctly (Asteral, 2011). Typically, one time initial training sessions are not sufficient enough for medical practitioners to operate increasingly complex medical equipment (World Health Organization, 2010). Training sessions can be carried out by specialists sent directly from the OEM, or they could be carried out by OEM certified professionals on the MES provider's retainer. In the latter case, the OEM must have enough market dominance and equipment volume to warrant keeping a team of OEM certified professional (i.e. the MES provider must have enough equipment to support the costs associated with keeping and OEM certified maintenance specialist) (Chan, 2003). The ultimate source of equipment knowledge and information is the OEM, however with support from the OEM (through training and certification), a 3rd party service provider such as an MES provider can have a maintenance and repair team that is highly competent (Kensett, 1990).

2.4.6 Insurance

Insurance is mandatory when purchasing expensive medical equipment. Insurance in a Managed Equipment Services contract covers the loss/ damage of equipment as well as employee or public third party liability. (Jin-Li & Yuan-Fu, 2004) The extent of the insurance coverage is covered in the contract to be signed between the MES and the medical facility. Insurance coverage is determined based on the requirements shown by the hospital/ trusts ensuring that the risk of safeguarding the medical equipment is transferred from the hospital/ trusts to the MES provider. (Asteral, 2011)

2.4.7 Asset Management

To meet the demands of quality patient care an accountable, efficacious, safe, cost-effective and systemic approach needs to be established. Such an approach ensures availability and manages the existing resources on a best-value equipment service. Additionally, the existing measurable management strategies need to be monitored and evaluated in this element.[4] This should include the documentation of equipment service costs, the in-house and possible external equipment service costs, extent of guarantee and warranty coverage for each inventory item, equipment-user operation schedule, quality of maintenance level for each item and ap-

[4] As defined under the Strategic alliance & management element.

propriateness of the service provider and reasonable maintenance costs. (David & Judd, 2000)

Hospitals maintain a huge inventory of equipment. Maintaining such comprehensive current database for medical equipment in the hospital is often difficult for personnel, as complications arise when attempting to track equipment movement, and maintenance history. Well established OEMs, like GE, Philips and Siemens invest heavily in obtaining the skills needed, not only to manufacture the equipment, but also for "product development, equipment design and installation, manufacturing process design and development, software, risk management, analytical method development, manufacturing, testing, quality assurance, distribution, and increasingly, product lifecycle and "green" issues resolution" (Lincoln, 2009, pp. 11-12) The MES provider has the expertise and technology to track the equipment, and maintain accurate records. MES providers perform routine equipment audits to ensure the accuracy of the information in the database. This frees hospital personnel for the time consuming duty of making inventory counts. (Cameron, 2003).

2.4.8 Performance & Safety Monitoring

A. Performance Monitoring:

An agreed upon equipment performance quota is stated in the terms of the MES contract; healthcare providers typically ask for a 98% performance guarantee during working hours. If the agreed upon levels of service are not reached, the service provider must pay financial penalties. (OEM Service Manger, 2011) The MES provider is typically required to provide detailed performance reports on a constant, periodic basis. The report should provide reasonable justifications for instances during which the agreed and actual performance levels do not coincide.

Defining the KPIs allows the parties to measure and evaluate their performance on an ongoing basis, and thereby identify methods through performance can be dramatically improved (Parmenter, 2010). Defining and evaluating the KPIs must be done in line with Strategic Alliance requirements and goals. As such it is the alignment, clarification and implementation of KPIs is vital to the success of an MES program.

B. Safety Monitoring:

Due to the complexity of advanced medical equipment and their invasive nature, there are many unexpected interactions that lead to accidents and injury. As a result, some of the medical equipment used is considered high-risk systems. Legal complications, high financial compensations, and loss of reputation are all risks associated with accidents related to equipment failure and misuse. (Dain, 2002) An MES provider ensures that the risks associated with equipment failure are substantially reduced by providing trained professionals who periodically perform critical equipment examination, safety checks, onsite medical technology experts, safety training hospital staff, and safety alerts (Egbert, 2009). In addition some MES providers have a remote equipment tracking system, through which an expert continuously monitors equipment for inconsistency, and sends immediate alerts notifying the parties responsible (Siemens AG, 2011).

Therewith, the safety monitoring is in addition to the performance monitoring not only important to justify, confirm and align. Moreover there are also country specific laws and regulatory that has to be ensured and therewith monitored. This often requires a deep knowledge that has to be continuously updated due to the ongoing optimization and change in the laws and regulations.

2.4.9 Maintenance

In consideration of the scope, range, and volume of the equipment, the MES provider will typically keep a primary-equipment-care team in the healthcare facility that will be in charge of all maintenance tasks; this includes daily management, and routine maintenance. Contracts are arranged to keep a steady supply of parts, and preventive maintenance with the relevant Original Equipment Manufacturer (OEM). (Asteral, 2011) The MES provider depending on its presence and size in the market will either have its own OEM certified equipment technicians, or it will coordinate with the OEM so that its technicians are readily available when needed (Lavy & Shohet, 2009). If the MES provider has a large presence in the market (i.e. the MES provider has a large volume of equipment from different OEMs), then the Provider may keep its own team of OEM certified professionals on standby. In this case the MES provider will act as an extended arm of the Service Centre of the OEM and could perform OEM specific tasks such as providing a warranty service, based on service agreements with the OEM.

Spare parts are thereby sourced from the OEM through the MES provider, guaranteeing high quality functionality. The team could also be responsible for performing heavy maintenance tasks, in which case, the team already consist of technicians who are trained and certified by the OEM. Having these certified technicians readily available substantially reduces equipment downtime, allowing for high patient turnover. Leicester Hospital NHS Trust for example achieved an uptime of over 99% across 170 items of major equipment (Asteral, 2011).

2.4.10 Technology adjustment

The main advantage of this element is reducing or eliminating the risks associated with technology obsolescence of the medical devices that comes from rapid technology introduction. Healthcare providers in the Middle East compete based on the advancement of the technology available, and such try to retain the most advanced equipment possible. An MES program might help reduce many of the risks associated with information technology obsolescence. This can only happen by the efficient, successful, and effective planning of the OEM which is undoubtedly able to conduct such a process (Liu, Yang, Yang, & Dai, 2008). As such high costs are incurred when these healthcare providers are forced to replace a piece of equipment that becomes out-dated before its time (Alpen Capital Limited, 2009). The MES provider ensures that the equipment installed has the flexibility to handle structural updates, and thereby lengthens the lifespan of the equipment. This is done by maintaining a transparent relationship with the relevant OEMs ensuring the feasibility of technology update inclusions (Asteral, 2011).

Health Technology Management (HTM) is a systematic process in which qualified health care professionals such as the medical engineers employed by the MES provider use their ability to visualize a wide range of systems issues and determine important linkages and solutions in partnership with the leading OEMs.

This is an important factor that essentially ensures the highest quality of care at the best costs. HTM typically begins with strategic planning, technology assessment and facility planning, technology procurement, and is followed by maintenance management. (Judd, 2004)

Quality assessment, improvement and reporting of technology consumes 20% or more of all health care capital and operational investments, at one of the largest private healthcare organization in the world and is a must in the 21st century (Judd, 2004). As such this element has a significant importance.

2.5 Benefits of MES

A typical MES program provides benefits to Patients, Insurance, OEMs and specially Clinical Staff and Trusts/ organization.

Synergies can be created between all the stakeholders. As an example, the users of the equipment, as well as the MES and the OEMs service engineers save time and effort with regards to monitoring and maintenance documentation. This means that the user/ healthcare provider is relieved of the responsibility of monitoring and documenting every detail and as such, can focus on the core business responsibility. This consequently improves departmental efficiency. Moreover the users are naturally without appropriate technical knowledge and therefore are unable to determine the appropriate level of service required for their equipment. This can lead to expensive service costs, unnecessary equipment repair, or even premature equipment replacement if the user needs to maintain the equipment on short notice. On the other hand this represents a benefit for the OEM since professional handling of the equipment is guaranteed at all times (Chan, 2003).

Traditionally each department within a healthcare facility deals independently with the service provider. The MES provider, who acts as a centralized arrangement, can negotiate for all the healthcare providers it is in contact with. With a large equipment volume, the MES provider can achieve economies of scale and thereby lower costs. Additionally, a successful MES program offers a decision making criteria not only for equipment procurement, but also for prioritizing the maintenance management decisions. This way both the MES provider and the hospital can save unnecessary costs that will eventually raise both of their margins (Taghipour, S; Banjevic, D; Jardine, A K S., 2011). Other benefits such as attaining priority for spare parts or updates can also be attained. Some of the benefits for the individual parties are described next (Chan, 2003).

Healthcare provider/ Clinical Staff:

Organizations or trusts outsource non-core activities to third party players in order to reduce risks, costs and to focus on their core functions. In addition they can increase the quality of the equipment portfolio. (Pathology In Practice, 2007) Along with the knowledge of the equipment, the MES provider offers a centralized equipment & service contact point, with the history (e.g. last service that was performed etc.) and experiences of each item, in detail. (Chan, 2003).

Therefore with MES, the hospital management can concentrate on their primary function of providing a high standard healthcare to patients, while the responsibility for the upkeep, maintenance, and integration of all the equipment can be transferred to the MES service provider. In addition, MES can drastically improve the image of the healthcare provider in terms of social responsibility. MES programs allow lowering wasted, and already scarce to begin with, resources. (Lindgreen, Antioco, & Harness, 2009) MES provides benefits for the clinicians, patients, and trusts. Patient benefits include: short waiting times, advanced equipment which improve safety and treatment, quick delivery, an improved hospital environment, reduced risk due to the regular equipment servicing and staff training, as well as swift procedures. MES ensures a guaranteed performance level as high as 99% during working hours which leads to high levels of productivity and improvement from clinicians. (Pathology In Practice, 2007)

Benefits to clinicians include improved highly focused patient care, improved working environment, up-to-date and well maintained - bug free -equipment, swifter budgetary planning, and low equipment downtime which leads to a better use of operator time and to higher return on investment. While MES is viewed as being very expensive by trusts that run the hospital in the short term, it does provide overriding long term benefits. Benefits to trusts involve: high long term savings, increased productivity and enhanced performance, lower downtime due to effective equipment utilization, guaranteed performance levels, and the transfer of risk to the MES provider allowing the clinic to focus on providing high quality services to the patients. The next table lists the advantages of having an MES program for the medical facility as opposed to independently maintaining and servicing medical equipment. (Asteral, 2011)

The main benefits of outsourcing maintenance to the MES provider (from the healthcare provider's perspective) are addressed in the table below. The benefits are derived from the Essential Equipment Services scheme.

	In-sourced by Healthcare Provider	Managed Equipment Service Provider
Procurement	Complex task with hidden risks (e.g. interface to existing system)	Substantially less complex due to existing experience and knowledge
Operational Cost	Substantially higher	Substantially lower
Cost Transparency	Numerous hidden costs	Fixed known cost
Cost Predictability	Fluctuating costs	Relatively stable fixed costs
Upgrade Costs	Additional or hidden costs	Generally or incorporated in contract
Quality Service	Inconsistent relies on fragmented procedures	Consistent/ OEM Certified/ Standardized
Skills	Variable skills, often uncertified by the manufacturer	OEM Certified and specialist
Flexibility	Relatively inflexible, heavily depends on availability of the healthcare provider's resources	Readily available resources; allows for rapid growth/ development
Standardization	Partly to none	Certified procedures and solid implementation based on best practices
Maintenance Specialists	Decentralist, multi OEM service contact points	Single point of contact, centrally managed

Table 1: Facility-Sourced Maintenance vs. MES (MES Survey, 2011) (Healthcare Provider 1, 2011) (Healthcare Provider 2, 2011)

The following describes in detail the advantages of MES for each stakeholder.

MES provider

The MES provider wants to maximize its profits by using an optimized business model. Initially, the provider needs to be more efficient in maintenance as well as managing healthcare equipment than the healthcare provider. Typically the MES provider can ensure this by using its knowledge and optimizing synergy effects which a typical healthcare provider may not be capable of. Synergy can be obtained through sharing resources, knowledge, and passing on bargaining power to one single point of contact. The MES provider can therefore purchase higher volumes of equipment and services from the OEM at a lower price. Another benefit is that the business model, by virtue of a long-term contract, ensures a stable business. (MES Provider 1, 2010)

OEM

To avoid dealing with multiple healthcare providers independently; the equipment manufacturer always has a high interest in collaborating with the MES provider. Due to the MES provider's large scale and scope of operations, the OEM communicates with one centralized entity to gain access to multiple healthcare experts and healthcare providers. The OEM therefore benefits by contracting multiple high volume single orders and achieves higher economies of scale and cost efficiency. (Chan, 2003)

Payer (Patient/ Insurer)

Both the patients and the insurance companies are interested in high quality safe treatments as well as in reducing healthcare expenses. MES contributes to effective standardized processes that ensure time efficient and non-complex procedures. This is a benefit that is highly important to both patients and insurance companies. (HC Consultancy 2, 2011)

Further insight on the benefits of MES is provided in a case study that can be found in the appendix and is published by a healthcare equipment provider.

2.6 Risks of MES

All parties undertake some amount of risk in an MES program. The risk carried on by the first party on behalf of the second party becomes an advantage to the second party and a disadvantage the first party and vice versa. In this section the key risk areas are identified and described for both MES provider and the healthcare provider.

Risks undertaken by the MES provider

An MES project transfers many risks which were previously healthcare provider's responsibility to the MES provider. For example, they have to keep track of the latest technologies; through an MES provider, equipment responsibility and the risks associated with it are taken away from the healthcare provider allowing healthcare professionals to focus on their core medical tasks. Potential risk areas such as rectifying faults which is a major problem for clinicians can be taken care of by the MES service provider. (Pathology In Practice, 2007)

Therefore the risks outsourced to the MES provider are an increase in the cost of equipment, the cost of spare parts or maintenance, the cost if rectifying faults, ensuring equipment availability/ uptime, correctly conducting of the safety notices and regularise including the accurate records of device history and training, being able to recruit and retain the right amount of experts, the correct building of specification, design and project management. The MES provider is at risk of paying high penalties to the healthcare provider if the agreed equipment uptime is not maintained. (Asteral, 2011)

Risks to the Healthcare provider

Outsourcing maintenance and especially management of healthcare equipment is risky as involves outsourcing people, functions, applications and processes in hope, that the MES provider can improve the overall competitiveness of the healthcare provider. Therefore one of the risks is the failure of the MES provider to meet the business objective and that he will fail below the expectations. Another key issue is the protection of intellectual property, especially the protection of confidential data and trade secrets. (Power, Desouza, & Bonifazi, 2006) A long-term contract means that there is an intensive dependence on the MES provider. If the MES provider is not able or willing to adapt to unforeseen changes needed changes that could not be included or foreseen at the beginning of the contract. (HC Consultancy 3, 2011)

2.7 MES SWOT

The SWOT analysis thoroughly evaluates the organisation by pinpointing its strengths, weaknesses, opportunities and threats (SWOT) (Subba Rao, 2010). As such this analysis is being used to assess the benefits and the risks described. SWOT enables the formulation of the right strategies for the business firm (Subba Rao, 2010). Therefore the analysis focuses on the MES provider but still takes in-to consideration the other stakeholders involved. The strengths identified are the skills, competencies, valuable organisation resources, competitive capabilities or achievements that give the MES provider competitive advantage and enables it to both achieve and exceed its goals. The weaknesses are aspects that are performed poorly in comparison to the existing standards and competitors. Opportunities are seen here as significant avenues for growth or for competitive advantages. The threats are environmental factors that pose place pressure on the MES provider and endangers its operations. (Subba Rao, 2010) Every element can have one or more aspects of this. However, only one typical result is described to demonstrate one scenario.

Strengths:

Usage of Synergies for the MES provider and the OEM:

Synergies can be created through the procurement process. The MES provider can group to wield more bargaining power towards the OEMs. This benefit he can pass on towards the medical provider with cheaper equipment prices. This again can be passed on from the medical provider to the patient and give both an access to economy of scale. (Chan, 2003)

Concentration on core business for the healthcare provider:

Focus is placed on Costs & Quality. The MES provider, as the equipment and maintenance expert, can focus on his speciality. This on the other hand gives the possibility to the medical provider to focus on this expertise. Based on his expertise he can to these tasks more efficient. On the other hand, the medical provider can focus more on increasing the quality of care instead of wasting time and therewith money by maintaining the equipment. In addition this gives a competitive advantage to the clinicians who can focus more intensively on the patient by working with more up to date equipment. As a whole, this will increase the efficiency and effectiveness and therewith the costs and quality and ensures adequate financial resources. (Judd, 2004)

Optimized stability towards costs, time & quality for the MES and healthcare provider:

E.g. based on the mentioned expertise from the MES provider he can evaluate and therefore ensure the time for maintenance services on the medical equipment better, as the medical provider could do with far less medical equipment knowledge. This also means that the MES provider will have more certified specialists and medical equipment experts. In addition the MES provider is ensured with a long-term stable income. The healthcare provider on the other hand can plan the costs for equipment and service better, since the provider has stable and transparent cost structure instead of fluctuating expenses. (MES Survey, 2011) (MES Provider 2, 2010)

Independence for MES and healthcare provider:

This strength focuses on the fact that the MES provider is more independent as the healthcare provider or any OEM. With this he can decide free from any reliance or favour the medical user might have, but which would not increase the quality or reduce the costs. (Chan, 2003) to focus on a special area or niche market. (OEM Service Manger, 2011) In this section some worldwide MES projects, which are run by large firms who generally dominating the MES business, are selected and explored.

2.8.1 Asteral Solutions

Asteral has launched three projects in the UK with cooperation of National Health Services (NHS).

Peterborough's and Stamford Hospital NHS Trust

This was the first MES contract signed in the UK between Asteral and National Hospital Service (NHS) of UK. The 33 year vendor independent contract is designed to lower operational costs and provide the latest technology and maintenance. High quality service and technology updates provided through a sustainable financial investment plan were key terms in the MES contract. (Asteral, 2011)

Whittington Hospital NHS Trust

Due to difficulties replacing its radiology equipment and financing of new equipment, Whittington Hospital awarded a 15 year MES contract in October 2005 to Asteral. The main purpose of the contract was to guarantee equipment servicing, and the feasibility of technology update inclusions. Under a fixed monthly payment system, Whittington Hospital now receives services that it could not have been able to afford nor effectively implement. (Whittington Health, 2011)
Through a Private Finance Initiative (PFI) model similar to a Public Private Partnership (PPP) model, Asteral provides Whittington Hospital with its financial as well as maintenance and servicing provisions.(Whittington Health, 2011)

University Hospital of Leicester (UHL)

Under a £761 million, 30 years (US$1.256 billion) PFI initiative, Asteral is responsible for managing UHL's imaging diagnostics facilities as well as for refurbishing the facilities with an MES setup. One of the unique aspects of this deal is that Asteral was bound to provide risk free service within the existing budget of the hospital, rather than devise a new one. Asteral developed a customized MES solution which provided UHL with a fulltime biomedical engineer and service staff along with the equipment at a fixed monthly cost. The benefits received by UHL are typical to those of an MES deal mentioned earlier in this dissertation. (Asteral, 2011)

2.8.2 Philips Healthcare

Philips Mediserve is the brand name for Philips Healthcare's MES service program key projects in the UK that are listed and described. Philips MediQuip offers end-to-end solutions.

A) Royal Belfast Hospital (Philips Mediserve)

Royal Belfast Hospital is one of the largest hospitals in Northern Ireland. The MES contract was negotiated for a period of 15 years under a PFI scheme. For a fixed annual fee, Philips will provide complete turnkey solutions for the hospital's imaging centre. According to the £25 million (US$41.26 million) deal, Philips also manages the clinical information systems (Philips, 2011).

B) Orbis Medical Centre (Philips Mediserve)

For a period of 20 years, under a vendor-independent deal, Philips acts as a single-point-of-contact for the hospital design, planning and implementation purposes. This contract also includes the integration of IT solutions for the hospital. Philips will provide refurbished as well as new medical devices for the hospital. (Philips, 2011)

C) Zambia Healthcare (Philips MediQuip)

Over a period of seven years (2002-2009), Philips executed a €25 million healthcare infrastructure project. Through a financial and strategic collaboration with the Dutch government, Philips provided diagnostic imaging and surgical services in Zambia. This project was done with financial and strategic assistance from the Dutch Government. Philips also took charge of training the locals in managing and maintaining the equipment to build a sustainable healthcare system through a unique program called "Training the Trainer" through which biomedical engineers would train new recruits. (Philips, 2011)

2.8.3 Siemens Healthcare

Siemens Healthcare, UK operates 11 MES projects. Below is a list and description of the company's major MES projects.

A) Bart's and London NHST Trust

Siemens signed a 35 year £300 million (US$495.3 million) deal with Bart's (owned by Capital Hospitals). Siemens is responsible for all aspects of medical diagnostic equipment care: financing, maintenance of medical diagnostic devices as well as user training. The deal has been described by the trust as being cost-effective and time saving. (Siemens AG, 2007)

B) Barnet Hospital

In 1999 Barnet Hospital commissioned Metier Healthcare consortium (led by Siemens, Bouygues and Ecovert) to build and run the hospital. The deal is now a PFI contract worth £128 million exclusive to Siemens for a period of 33 years. Siemens provides equipment installation, maintenance, and upgrading services Siemens is also responsible for the over 2500 pieces of various medical equipment, in addition to the hospital's telecommunications facilities and its MRI scanning service. (Siemens AG, 2007)

C) Queens Hospital, Romford

In 2003, Siemens secured a £393 million (US$648.8 million) PFI scheme MES contract for a period of 33 years through Catalyst Healthcare (the consortium responsible for the project). The contract encompasses the supply, maintenance and management of all equipment (4,000 pieces of equipment) for Queens Hospital (Siemens AG, 2004).

3. Medical Equipment Services Approach and Design

As described in the previous chapter, achieving the highest level of equipment operational efficiency requires knowledge of brand's design, mechanics, weaknesses, and operational efficiency, as well as other technical aspects that only an OEM would have knowledge of. Achieving high levels of efficiency using internal staff would be especially difficult if the healthcare provider has multiple equipment brands for the same type of device. According to Anthony Chan in his book Medical Technology Management Practice, "It is undesirable to have different makes and models of one type of equipment…", standardization of equipment results in, "Increased operational efficiency due to familiarity of the device…decreased operating hours… reduced training costs" (Chan, 2003, p. 114). It would be very difficult for a healthcare provider to have the same equipment brand without replacing the facility's current equipment, and thereby incur unnecessary equipment replacement risks. An OEM certified MES professional would allow the healthcare provider to reap the benefits of equipment standardization due to their expert knowledge and familiarity with the brand experts in the equipment brand that they are responsible for. In this section, the procedure used to design the model is described. The models were designed from the MES provider's perspective, taking into consideration the needs of the healthcare provider as well as of the other stakeholders. (Zeithaml, 2009)

3.1 MES Stakeholders

In relation to the MES equipment service portfolio, four main stakeholders are to be considered within the Stakeholder Framework of an MES model: the healthcare provider, the MES provider, the OEM, and the Financing entity (Dunham-Taylor & Pinczuk, 2010).

Figure 3: MES Stakeholders

The MES Provider:

Based on information attained through collective primary and secondary research techniques, MES providers can be defined as businesses that are both medical equipment vendors who also have extensive experience in equipment management and associated services equipment management services, or those who are only service providers offering their services to healthcare providers for a periodic fee. MES Providers tend to have a strong financial standing and a large presence in the market (HC Consultancy 2, 2011) (OEM, 2011) (MES Survey, 2011).

Healthcare Provider:

Healthcare is the practice concerned with the maintenance of health and the prevention, alleviation, or cure of disease (Encyclopædia Britannica, 2011). A healthcare provider is a business entity that delivers medical services to people in need of healthcare. Within an MES framework, however the healthcare provider according to the research conducted needs to be comparatively large in terms of the size of its long-life medical equipment portfolio.

Financing Entity:

There are a number of financing entities that could be used to finance equipment purchases. These include commercial banks, sales finance companies, equipment sellers, insurance companies, equipment vendors, insurance companies and pension funds (Akintoye & Chinyio, 2005). Within the context of an MES program, the MES provider is also to be included within this list (Moyer, McGuigan, & Kretlow, 2009).

Original Equipment Manufacturer:

The original equipment manufacturer of medical equipment is a business entity that produces complex equipment (such as medical equipment) from components usually bought from other manufacturers and sells the equipment under its own brand name either directly, or through an independent vendor (Encyclopædia Britannica, 2011). Due to the fact that an MES program is more effective for more expensive medical equipment with a relatively long lifetime, the original equipment manufacturer is generally one that produces such equipment (Asteral, 2011).

3.2 Ownership Schemes

3.2.1 No Ownership

Essentially under this scheme, the MES provider acts only as a service provider and is not responsible for the equipment procurement financing aspect of operations. Therefore, all risks associated with the contract are borne only from the services that the MES provider is in control of (Hardy, 2004).

As the equipment would be on the healthcare provider's balance sheet, all equipment associated liabilities (i.e. depreciation) would be the responsibility of the healthcare provider. In addition, if the healthcare provider acquired the equipment through a loan from a financing entity, then the healthcare provider would undertake the payment default risks. The healthcare provider would own all of the equipment risks, with exception to the equipment's replacement risk if stipulated in the contract. Equipment risk is evaluated based on equipment functional risk, physical risk, and maintenance risk. The healthcare provider however would have full control over how the equipment is operated, when it can be sold or disposed of and all revenues (Nah & Osifo-Dawodu, 2007).

According to interviews conducted, if the MES provider is in charge of equipment planning, due to the provider's expertise, and knowledge of the product market equipment quality risk is removed. If however this MES provider is not responsible for equipment planning (in the essential services scheme) then the healthcare provider would have to bear the equipment quality risks. Based on the ownership scheme chosen, the MES provider would bear equipment replacement risk and equipment interface compatibility risk (OEM MES Provider, 2011).

3.2.2 Financing Ownership Scheme

The Financing Ownership Scheme involves higher risk intakes by the MES provider than the No Ownership Scheme. Equipment financing may be obtained from banks, financing companies (usually a subsidiary of the manufacturer), and manufacturers of the equipment (Shim & Siegel, 2009). Under this scheme, the funds for the equipment are given as a loan from the MES provider to the healthcare provider. Either the MES provider's own financial resources are used to procure the equipment, or the MES provider obtains a loan from a financing entity and uses it to purchase the equipment for the healthcare provider. In the latter case, the healthcare provider would pay back the MES provider in periodic instalments (Sacher & Louis, 1998).

According to Richards C. Osborn in *Business Finance the Management Approach*, "Part of the high cost of equipment financing…stems from the fact that small firms with limited credit are restricted in their own source of funds and have slight bargaining power, they depend on the manufacturer or dealer to handle the sale of the equipment to finance that sale or to at least arrange the financing" (Osborn, 1965, p. 252). Within an MES Financing Ownership scheme, the MES provider steps in using its high credit standing and large market presence to negotiate and arrange the financing required at attractive interest rates. The financing entity and the healthcare provider both benefit from having the MES provider as an intermediary. If the financing entity is a bank or a financing company, then both the bank and the healthcare provider benefit; the healthcare provider benefits from attaining attractive interest rates, and the bank benefits by reducing its risk when giving a loan to a larger entity whose risk is diversified over a large number of customers (Gulácsi, Dávid, & Dózsa, 2002).

According to interviews conducted with multiple MES providers, under an MES framework, the seller in this situation is considered to be the MES provider, if the healthcare provider buys directly from the MES provider using the MES provider's owns equipment. If the equipment is financed through a loan from a financing institution (acquired by the MES provider) then the seller is considered to be the financing institution and the buyer is both the MES provider and the healthcare provider. This is true as the cost of the instalments paid to the financing institution by the MES provider is passed off to the healthcare provider (OEM, 2011).

Equipment financing is usually acquired through a purchase loan instalment. The benefit of this form of financing is that the equipment can outlive the cost benefits of a lease (Nichols & Day, 2010). The two most popular forms of this financing method are a chattel mortgage and a conditional sales contract (Shim & Siegel, 2009). In both cases the buyer, pays the seller in fixed instalments. A chattel mortgage is generally defined as "A loan for which certain items of inventory are other moveable property serve as collateral"; in this case the borrower retains ownership of the equipment when the contract is signed, but cannot sell the equipment without the consent of the lender (Garman & Forgue, 2009) (Longenecker, Moore, Palich, & Petty, 2006). The borrower repays the lender in periodic instalment as well as an agreed upon interest rate. While the borrower has legal claim to the equipment, the borrower cannot sell the equipment without the lender's consent (Van Horne & Wachowicz, 2005). The lender may repossess the equipment and resell it if the borrower defaults on the loan payment (Moyer, McGuigan, & Kretlow, 2009). A chattel mortgage benefits the lender, as the borrower immediately retains ownership to the equipment and as such it must be placed on the borrower's balance sheet. If the loan is directly sourced from the MES provider, the MES provider benefits by transferring equipment ownership risks to the healthcare provider (ownership risks transferred are based on the terms/ services agreed upon in the contract). If the MES provider acquires the equipment through a loan from a financing entity, then the MES provider takes-up more risk. The healthcare provider benefits retaining immediate ownership and therefore control of the equipment. As such the healthcare provider can avoid risks such as technology obsolescence by selling the equipment if the lender (either the MES provider or the financing entity through the MES provider) agrees. Mortgages are an advantage to both the borrower and the lender if the lender is the MES provider. According to Jae K. Shim and Joel G. Siegel, "Mortgages have several benefits such as favourable interest rates, fewer financing restrictions..., extended maturity dates for repayment, and easy availability" (Shim & Siegel, 2009, p. 350). Due to the fact that the MES provider does not have ownership and has very few risks, the chattel mortgage is placed on the lower end of the ownership range in the x-axis (Ownership) of the Portfolio/ Ownership (POM) Matrix.

A conditional sales contract is almost exclusively used by equipment sellers. In a conditional sales contract (between the OEM and the MES provider or between the healthcare provider and the MES provider), the seller of the equipment (the OEM via the MES provider or the OEM directly) keeps the title to the equipment until the buyer (the healthcare provider or the MES provider) fulfils all of the periodic instalments and terms agreed upon in the contract. This is similar to a leasing agreement except that while under a lease agreement, the right to ownership is optional (decided when the last payment is due). The difference is that under a conditional sales contract the ownership must be transferred to the buyer when all payments are made (Jacobus, 2008). A conditional sales contract guarantees that ownership costs and the risk of technology obsolescence will be passed on to the healthcare provider at the end of the contract period and thus benefits the healthcare provider. Hence, the conditional sales agreement is placed on the higher end of the Finance Ownership range in the x-axis (Ownership) of the Portfolio/ Ownership (POM) Matrix.

The MES provider would also benefit by keeping title to the equipment, and therefore would avoid the legal costs associated with repossessing ownership of the equipment and foreclosure. In addition, the MES Provider also benefits, as maintenance and operational costs of the equipment are owned by the healthcare provider. As long as the healthcare provider pays the required instalments, the healthcare provider would benefit by having equitable right to the equipment (guaranteed ownership) at the end of the contract period. (Jacobus, 2008) Moreover, the healthcare provider also benefits because ownership costs such as depreciation are recorded on the MES provider's balance sheet. (MES Provider 2, 2010) The repayment schedule of the loan is usually kept in line with the depreciation of the medical equipment to guarantee that the market value of the equipment exceeds the balance of the loan. In most cases the instalments are of equal value, the MES provider/ financing entity would benefit as the interest and the instalment margin gained represents a safety margin against depreciation risks (Van Horne & Wachowicz, 2005). Repossession of the equipment that is secured as part of this contract is subject to the legal regulations in the country (HC Consultancy 1, 2011).

3.2.3 Leasing Ownership Scheme

In this case the MES provider temporarily owns the equipment until it is transferred to the healthcare provider at the end of contract. For a leasing agreement to work, the term of the lease must be shorter than the lifetime of the equipment (Nevitt & Fabozzi, 2000). As the name suggests, under the lease model, the healthcare provider can lease equipment from the MES provider for a specific period of time. There are two types of leases that can be employed under this scheme: a capital lease and an operating lease. Operating leases last for a fraction of the duration of the asset, and are usually used as a substitute for capital leases. They generally have a shorter timeframe. During the lease period, the ownership of the equipment remains with the lessor (MES provider). An operating lease does not need to be capitalized as equivalent to debt on the balance sheet of the lessee (healthcare provider) if the lease lasts less than 75% of the useful life of an investment. As such, operating leases are preferred by small capacity healthcare providers and those with low purchasing power. Due to their shorter duration and easy cancellation provisions, operating leases are also preferred by healthcare providers that want the flexibility to easily change their equipment whenever technologically improvements arise (Pehlchen, 2003). This also makes them suitable for large medical equipment of lower value i.e. an x-ray machine. Their short duration make operating leases suitable for equipment that have shorter life times (Contino, 2006).

The healthcare provider under the operating lease can either make one time full payment or the healthcare provider can pay periodically. If the healthcare provider chooses to pay periodically, then the payment must be classified as an expense in the hospital's balance sheet (Englard, 2007). Operating leases benefit the healthcare provider as the equipment can be returned to the MES provider at any time if due notice is given. Since operating leases are only placed as an expense in the healthcare provider's income statement, the healthcare provider does not own any of the equipment liabilities, or its depreciation. In addition, the healthcare provider has the option to buy the equipment at the end of the lease which allows the healthcare provider to use the equipment for a long time, allowing the healthcare provider to make a more informed purchase decision (Weltman & Raeburn, 2007).

A capital lease (also known as a financial lease) is a long term lease that runs for most of the equipment's life time. In a capital lease, the lessor pays for the equipment, provides the required maintenance. The equipment is treated as an asset in the lessee's financial sheet and depreciation is expensed. The cash flow from the equipment during the term of the contract is sufficient to pay back the lessor's (MES provider) investment (Brigham & Houston, 2009). A capital lease is more suitable for equipment that has a long life time and high cost, i.e. MRI scanner. Ownership of the equipment is transferred to the lessee at the end of the contract at an agreed upon market price. Since the term of the lease covers most of the life time of the healthcare provider equipment, the lessee bears the risk of equipment obsolescence, once ownership is transferred to the lessee. At the end of the term of the lease, the healthcare provider must pay the residual value stipulated in the contract. Most capital leases have high default penalties, in order to ensure that the final payment is made. Due to its high capital requirements, a capital lease is suitable for high capacity healthcare provider with secure and high purchasing power. Therefore, a capital lease is often used in a PPP model in which a government entity provides the security which ensures that the required payments are made. Under a capital lease, all equipment risks are borne by the healthcare provider (Contino, 2006). Leases are therefore placed on the higher end of the ownership range due to the complexity and risks involved (Taylor, 2006). This is illustrated in the subsequent figure (Portfolio/ Ownership (POM) Matrix).

3.2.4 Rent (Full Ownership Scheme)

Under the rent ownership scheme, the equipment is rented to the healthcare provider at a fair market value (Taylor, 2006). The MES provider has permanent full ownership of the equipment under the MES contract, and thus undertakes all of the ownership risks related to the equipment. This scheme is very advantageous to the healthcare provider compared to the MES provider as all risks are owned by the MES provider (Maine, 2003). Under this scheme, the healthcare provider has no initial capital expenditure and that the latest equipment is guaranteed (Nichols & Day, 2010). The healthcare provider's stake in the relationship is very low; renting signifies a shorter tem MES contract, as a healthcare provider would rent equipment if it has not interest in owning or using it in the future. The advantages of renting for the healthcare provider include lower inventory, reduced need for internal maintenance staff, simpler accounting methods, and significant saving in insurance premiums (Pratt, 2011).

3.3 MES Model Design Approach

The process, resulting in the formation of the models, is described in this section. Based on the two crucial terms that must be determined in the MES contract, two key considerations were taken as the foundation upon which the models were designed; the level of equipment risk ownership and the scope of the services to be included in the contract.

MES services outlined in the *MES Process and Design* section of this paper were grouped according to the scope of the services provided and their relative importance to the healthcare provider. The level of the MES provider's ownership over the medical equipment that falls under the MES program was weighed and ownership schemes were identified. These two key factors were then plotted on a graph. The services were plotted as a range on the vertical axis from the most essential services to the least essential services. The level of ownership was plotted on the horizontal axis from lowest level of ownership by the MES provider (no ownership) to the highest level of ownership (full ownership) (Kimber, Jones, & Cornwell, 1983).

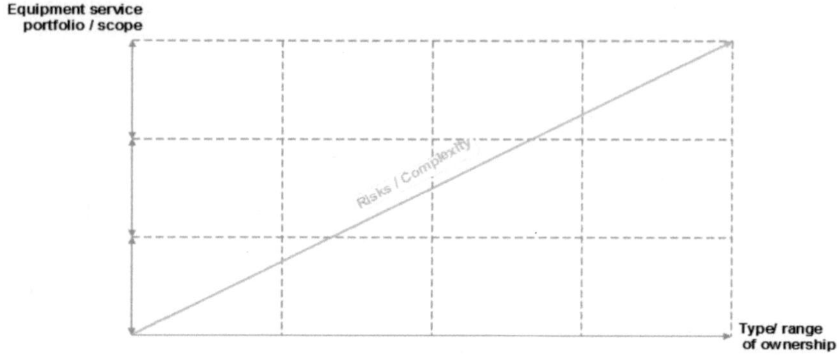

Figure 4: Ownership/ Services Matrix (HC Consultancy 2, 2011) (HC Consultancy 3, 2011) (HC Consultancy 4, 2011)

Three levels or groups of service were identified and bundled as conceptual portfolio offerings. Under "Essential Equipment Services", the most crucial equipment services were included. The Essential Equipment Services Scheme was devised based on the assumption that the healthcare facility has the necessary equipment planning and management knowledge but lacks the technical knowledge required to perform the core equipment care tasks (Davidson, 1986). Therefore, as illustrated in the next figure, six services were included under the Essential Equipment Services Scheme: Strategic Alliance and Management (1), Equipment Implementation (4b), User Training (5), Asset Manage ment (7), Performance Monitoring (8b) and Maintenance (9).

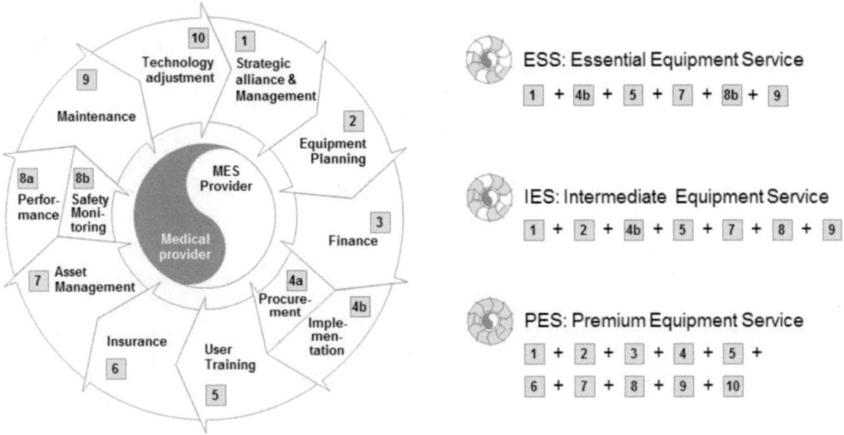

Figure 5: Service Paradigm (HC Consultancy 2, 2011) (Director 2, 2011) (Director 3, 2011)

The second group identified as the "Intermediate Equipment Services" include both the most essential services and ones that could ideally be outsourced by the healthcare provider to the MES provider in order to ease the pressure of some of the operational equipment responsibilities. The Intermediate Equipment Service Group as illustrated in the figure above includes the Strategic Alliance and Management (1), Equipment planning (2) Equipment Implementation (4b), User Training (5), Asset Management (7), Safety monitoring (8a), Performance Monitoring (8b) and Maintenance (9). The third group, the "Premium Equipment Services" includes the full scope of MES services; this group was founded based upon assumption that medical equipment responsibilities will be completely outsourced to the MES provider. As illustrated in the figure in the previous page, all of the services offered through an MES program were incorporated into the Premium Equipment Services group (OEM MES Provider, 2011) (OEM, 2011).

Four main ownership schemes based on the research conducted (Described in the *MES Ownership Schemes* subsection of this section) that could be adapted for an MES programs were identified and plotted on the x-axis. The first ownership scheme assumes that the MES provider has no legal ownership of the equipment or of the associated equipment risks; this constitutes the "No Ownership" scheme.

The second ownership scheme assumes that the MES provider owns the risks associated with equipment financing but not any of the other ownership risks; this scheme was identified and plotted as the “Financing Ownership” scheme on the x-axis. The third scheme assumes that the MES provider has temporary but full ownership of the medical equipment; therefore, the MES provider shares the ownership risks with the hospital; this was identified and plotted as the “Lease Ownership” scheme on the x-axis. The fourth scheme assumes that the MES provider permanently owns all of the equipment ownership risks. This scheme was identified as the “Full Ownership” major point on the x-axis. Under an MES contract, each ownership scheme for each device can vary, for example the MES provider can lease a CT and request financing assistance for an MR.[5]

The service groups were then plotted as major points on the y-axis, and the ownership schemes were plotted as major points on the x-axis as illustrated in the figure below.

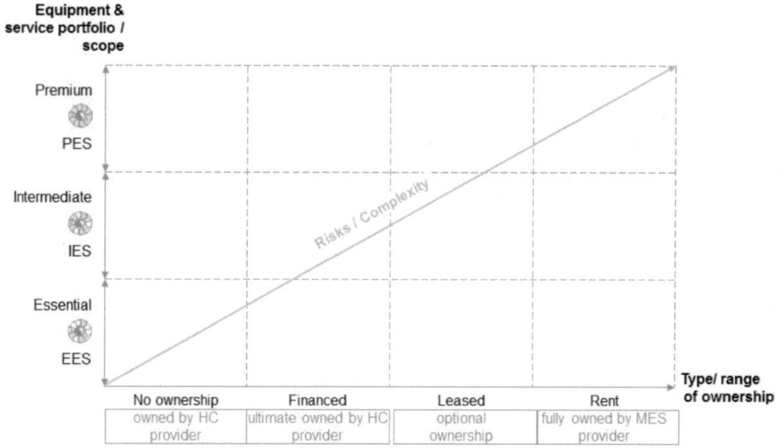

Figure 6: Portfolio/ Ownership Matrix[6]

---

[5] Based on multiple interviews with MES providers, for example see (HC Consultancy 2, 2011), (HC Consultancy 2, 2011)) and health consultants and senior government health officials.

[6] Own graph based on analysis of primary and secondary research results.

The meeting points of the major points of the x-axis and the y-axis on the graph above were taken as potential MES models. Twelve possible models were thus generated as provided in the figure below.

1. No Ownership, Essential Equipment Services
2. No Ownership, Operational Equipment Services
3. No Ownership, Premium Equipment Services
4. Financial Ownership, Essential Equipment Services
5. Financial Ownership, Operational Equipment Services
6. Financial Ownership, Premium Equipment Services
7. Lease Ownership, Essential Equipment Services
8. Lease Ownership, Operational Equipment Services
9. Lease Ownership, Premium Equipment Services
10. Full Ownership, Essential Equipment Services
11. Full Ownership, Operational Equipment Services
12. Full Ownership, Premium Equipment Services

These models are essentially options that can be offered by the MES provider as part of the provider's portfolio. As the ownership of the MES provider increases, the risks associated with the ownership increase due to the level of financial and legal liability the MES provider holds. In addition, as the number of services increase along with the human, physical resources, the complexity of coordinating the project especially in regards to the Strategic Alliance and Management service increases. (MES Provider 1, 2010) (Pehlchen, 2003)

Thus, the Full Ownership, Premium Equipment Services scheme is the most complex and the riskiest model, while the No Ownership Essential Equipment Services is the least complex and holds the least risk.

3.4 MES Stakeholder Framework

Within an MES framework, there are several possible relationships between the MES provider and the healthcare provider (OEM MES Provider, 2011). The MES provider could act as a:

- Equipment service provider- the equipment is not purchased from the OEM.
- 1st party financer of medical equipment and associated services – the equipment is financed directly using its own resources.
- 2nd party financer of the medical equipment and associated services – the MES provider finances the equipment via a financing entity.
- 2nd party financer of medical equipment and the equipment services – the MES provider finances the equipment via the original equipment manufacturer (UAE Government, 2011).

In conjunction with interviews conducted with MES providers, health consultants and doctors, four operational/ and financing scenarios were generated from the four relationships and the stakeholders identified (HC Consultancy 3, 2011). In designing these scenarios, three factors were taken into consideration and then mapped on to the MES Stakeholder framework:

1. Equipment procurement methods
2. The processes/ tasks that are performed
3. The transfer of funds/ payments

An additional stakeholder was added to the framework: the payer.

The payer according to the interviews conducted is either the patient (directly or through another individual), the insurer (for full coverage) or a combination of the patient and the insurance company depending on the extent of the insurance coverage that the patient has (Holdford & Brown, 2010). The relationship between the stakeholders is described in terms of financing and the operations. The dashed line refers to process/ task flow and the solid line refers to the direction of the flow of payments.

In the first scenario, (illustrated in the figure below) according to the survey and research conducted, the healthcare provider finances the equipment either using its own resources or through the OEM. In both cases, the MES provider does not own any of the ownership costs related to the equipment. The equipment is recorded either on the balance sheet of the healthcare provider or on the balance sheet of the OEM, depending on the ownership/ financing scheme (described later in this section) used (Pooler, Pooler, & Farney, 2004). As illustrated in the next figure, after an assessment of the healthcare provider's equipment needs, the MES provider communicates to the healthcare provider about the healthcare provider's equipment requirements. The healthcare provider purchases the equipment using its own resources (one time payment), or the through a lease/ loan from the OEM. In the latter case, the healthcare provider would pay back the OEM through periodic instalments (HC Consultancy 2, 2011) (UAE Government, 2011). Once the equipment is purchased and installed, the OEM authorizes the MES provider to take-up the equipment services that are under the equipment warranty. The MES provider in return communicates with the OEM if the OEM's assistance is needed (e.g. spare parts, repair, maintenance etc.). The MES provider grants the services agreed upon the MES contract and the healthcare provider in return uses patient revenue generated from the equipment (treatment revenue) to repay the MES provider for the services in periodic fixed/variable payments (fixed or variable as agreed upon in the contract) (Nah & Osifo-Dawodu, 2007). The process described in the second scenario is illustrated in the next figure.

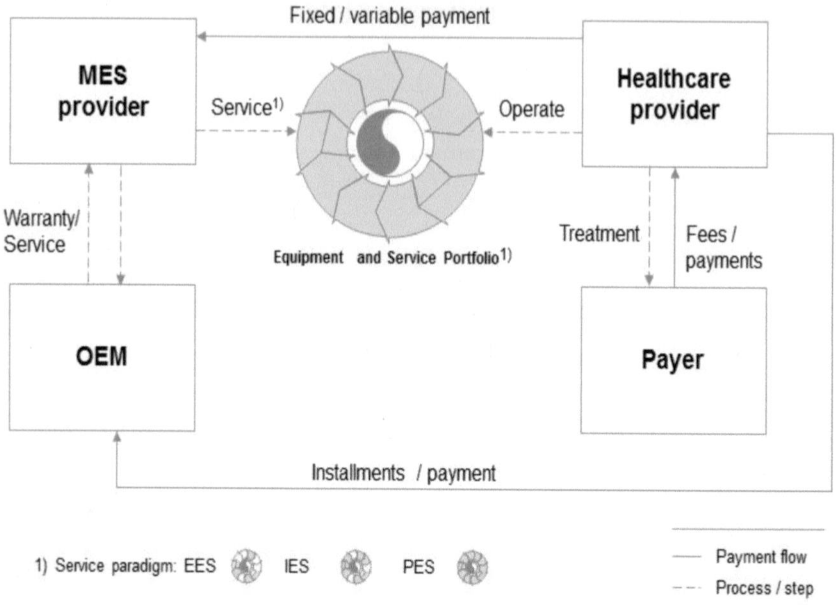

Figure 7: Stakeholder Framework: Healthcare Provider or OEM (HC Consultancy 2, 2011) (OEM MES Provider, 2011)

In the second scenario, the healthcare provider acquires the equipment through a loan/ lease from a financing entity such as a commercial bank or sales finance company. The financing entity pays the capital required to OEM to purchase the equipment. The OEM then installs the equipment and authorizes the MES provider to assume responsibility for the equipment services that are included in both the equipment warranty and the MES contract. The MES provider in return communicates with the OEM if the OEM's assistance is needed. The MES provider supplies the equipment services agreed upon to the healthcare provide. In turn, the healthcare provider pays the MES provider fixed instalments using the patient treatment/ care revenue generated from the equipment under the contract (HC Consultancy 2, 2011) (OEM, 2011) (UAE Government, 2011).

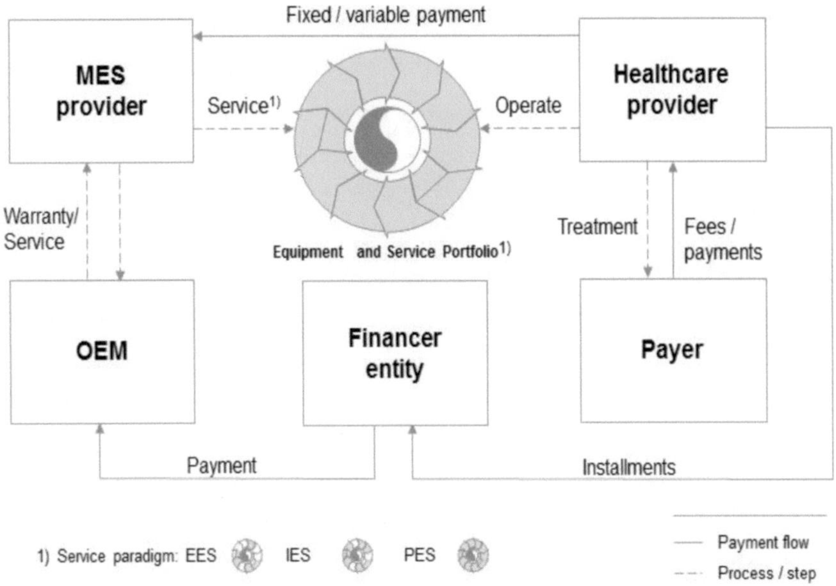

Figure 8: Stakeholder Framework: Healthcare Provider or Financing Entity (UAE Government, 2011)

In the third scenario, the healthcare facility requests that the MES provider to purchase the equipment either using its own financial resources or via the OEM. The MES provider thus acquires the equipment from the OEM by either using its own capital to finance the equipment or by virtue of a lease/ loan instalment from the OEM. In the latter case, the MES provider would incorporate the cost of the instalment and the interest into the cost structure of the payments that the healthcare provider would make to MES provider in order to cover the cost of the instalment paid to the OEM (OEM, 2011). The OEM delivers the equipment to the healthcare provider. For the periodic variable/ fixed payments made to MES provider, the healthcare provider receives the services agreed upon in the contract (Nevitt & Fabozzi, 2000). Payments to the MES provider are made via the revenue generated from the fees paid by the payer (insurer/ patient) for the treatment/ care received by using the equipment under the MES contract. The MES provider would then contact the OEM if its assistance is required to perform the MES services that are under both the equipment warranty and the MES contract. The processes described in the third scenario are illustrated in the next figure.

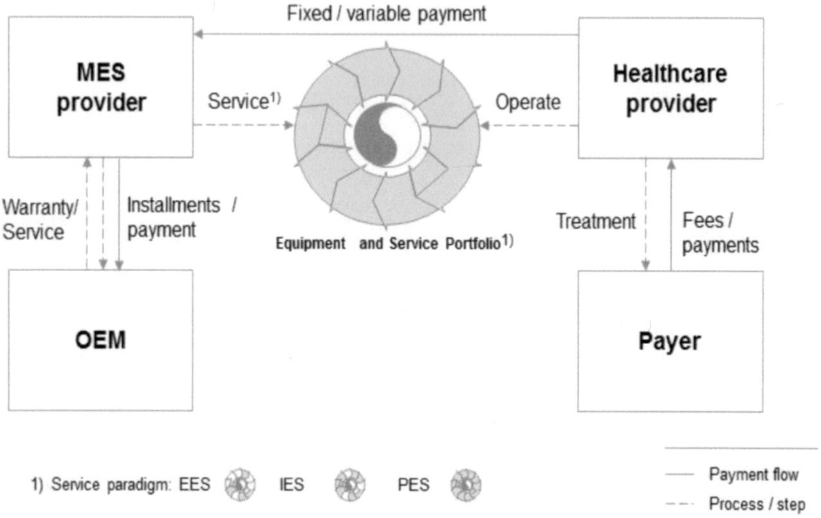

Figure 9: Stakeholder Framework: MES provider or OEM (UAE Government, 2011)

In the fourth scenario, the MES provider acquires the equipment financing from a financing entity for the healthcare provider in accordance with the equipment needs identified. The financing entity gives the OEM the payments required to purchase the equipment. The OEM then installs the equipment and authorizes MES provider to execute the services under both the warranty and the MES contract (as agree upon). The MES provider then pays the financing entity in installments that are incorporated into the periodic cost structure of the fixed/ variable fee that the healthcare provider pays the MES provider (UAE Government, 2011). The healthcare provider uses patient revenue generated from the use of the equipment.

3.5 MES Pricing Schemes

The healthcare provider pays the MES provider either a fixed fee or a variable fee based on patient flow. The profitability of either of these options is calculated using break-even analysis according to the Dictionary of Health Insurance and Managed Care, a break-even analysis within a healthcare delivery frame work, is an "Approach to analyze health care revenue, costs, and volume. It is based on production or medical service costs between those that are variable (change when output changes) and those that are fixed (not directly related to volume)" (Marcinko, 2006, p. 43).

3.5.1 Fixed Price

A fixed or a flat fee as illustrated in the next figure (Line A) is one that does not vary with the level of production (Gruen & Howarth, 2005). Paying a fixed fee bears more advantages to the MES provider than it does to the healthcare provider. A fixed fee ensures that the MES provider's fixed costs related to the contract are completely covered and a relatively constant profit margin is attained. A fixed fee essentially protects the MES provider from fluctuations in patient turnover for the equipment (Sihler, Crawford, & Davis, 2004). Fixed asset turnover or in this case medical equipment turnover is a measure of how effectively medical equipment is used. Equipment turnover is a ratio of the equipment's revenue to the value of the equipment (Swamidass, 2000). Therefore, the ratio of the equipment's revenue per patient to the cost of the equipment (derived from the value of the instalment per patient and other costs) is calculated to identify the number of patents required to break even and make a profit. Assuming that the cost of the fixed fee is partially or fully passed off to the patient, the healthcare provider profits only if the patient turnover rate generates enough income to fully cover the fixed costs related to operating the equipment (Level of Fixed costs in the next graph), as well as the cost of the fixed fee or to cover the part of the fixed fee that is passed over to patients (Huizenga, 2004) (Gruen & Howarth, 2005). The healthcare provider therefore would need to have a very consistent turnover rate in order to break even. If the turnover rate fluctuates negatively, the healthcare providers would incur losses (Gapenski, 2004). A fixed fee would negatively impact the payer (patients and insurers) as it is expected that healthcare provider would charge higher fees to ensure that the full or partial cost of the fixed fee is guaranteed at minimum patient turnover rate.

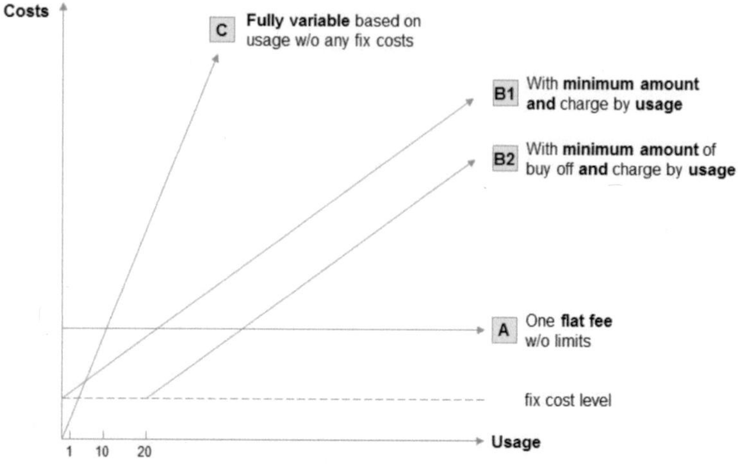

Figure 10: Pricing Schemes (HC Consultancy 2, 2011) (UAE Government, 2011) (OEM MES Provider, 2011)

3.5.2 Variable Price

A variable fee (Line C in the figure above) is classified as a variable cost under the healthcare provider's income statement and is defined as a cost that varies with the level of production. Taking into perspective the healthcare provider's point of view within the scope of an MES program, production refers to the number of patients within a particular period of time (Gruen & Howarth, 2005). A variable fee that wholly depends on patient flow and turnover is very advantageous to the healthcare provider as the healthcare provider would only pay per use. Therefore, the healthcare provider does not bear the risk of patient turnover fluctuations (as long as other fixed costs are covered) (Brigham & Ehrhardt, Financial Management Theory and Practice, 2009). According to Eugene F. Brigham, and Michael C. Ehrhardt in *Financial Management Theory and Practice*, "By using a per procedure…the hospital is converting a fixed cost for the equipment into a variable cost and thereby reducing the machines operating leverage, and therefore its break-even point" (Brigham & Ehrhardt, Financial Management Theory and Practice, 2009, p. 752). In contrast the MES provider's profits are susceptible to negative turnover rate fluctuations, and as such the model is more disadvantageous to the MES provider under such a payment scheme. Ideally, a wholly variable payment scheme is one that bears the highest benefit to the patient as the risk incurred by the healthcare provider is low and the healthcare provider would not raise its fees. The MES provider may attempt to compensate for patient fluctuation risks by charging a higher fee per use which would negatively impact both the payer (patients and insures) and the healthcare provider.

A combination pay per use payment scheme may also be used (Line B1 and B2 in the graph in the previous page). These would be classified as a semi-variable expense in the healthcare provider's income statement. Essentially, according to Reinhold Gruen, and Ann Howarth in *Financial Management in Health Services,* semi-variable costs/ expenses (for the healthcare provider) or semi-variable revenue (for the MES provider) is generated when "resources incur a standing charge that is payable regardless of whether the input is used plus a variable cost when activity increases" (Gruen & Howarth, 2005). One option (Line B1 in the figure in the previous page) is for the healthcare provider to pay a fixed fee for an agreed upon number usage occurrences and then make additional variable payments based on patient flow if the existing patient flow exceeds the fixed payment minimum. According to an interview conducted with the CEO of a healthcare consulting company, a second option for the healthcare provider is to pay the MES provider for the fixed cost of the equipment incurred from operations, as well as variable fee based on the usage occurrences of the equipment (OEM MES Provider, 2011). This payment plan is very advantageous to the MES provider as it covers both the MES provider's fixed fee along with a constant profit margin, as well as the opportunity to make extra profits from positive fluctuations in the healthcare provider's turnover rates. In contrast, the healthcare provider only receives the advantages of the variable payment scheme and misses out on the advantages of achieving a high turnover rate and economies of scale. When costs under these three payments schemes are fully passed off to the patient, the patient would have to pay higher fees to the healthcare provider. Assuming that the patient is insured, continuously increasing fees would raise the overall insurance premium offered to the patient and accordingly would have an overall high negative effect on the patient and healthcare demand.

3.6 Financial Statement Models

This subsection of the dissertation presents financial statements that could be used by a potential MES provider to assess the profitability of providing an MES program.

3.6.1 Cash Flow Statement

A cash flow statement is a record of net cash inflows and outflows by accounts or groups of accounts during the period reviewed and the net difference between the inflows and outflows during the period (Costales & Szurovy, 1994). A cash flow statement can be prepared to analyze the different applications and sources of cash, thus allowing the healthcare provider to make decisions regarding how to utilize its cash (MadeGowda, 2007, p. 367). The healthcare provider can then decide on the minimum level of cash required to operate the equipment and prevent recording a loss. The MES provider in turn can use this minimum in order to devise a pricing strategy, such as pricing scheme B2, in Pricing Schemes Graph.

Cash flow components

Cost of the Equipment/ Cost of Goods Sold (COGS)
COGS includes all the costs incurred in the process generating the medical equipment and providing it to the hospital; manufacturing, transportation, or installation of the device in the hospital (Weaver & Weston, 2008). The factors included in the COGS depend on the extent of the responsibility and ownership that MES provider has, i.e. the installation costs may be taken up by the MES provider rather than by the hospital.

Selling expenses
Selling expenses include all the expenses incurred as a result of the activities required to sell a product or service (Costales & Szurovy, 1994).

Administrative expenses

Any expense incurred as part of general administration for the equipment required. Administrative expenses are often grouped with selling expenses in absence of a clear distinction between the activities (Costales & Szurovy, 1994).

Training costs

Costs of training hospital staff to use the equipment. Depending on the training scheme agreed upon the contract, the activities included under a training expense will vary (Weaver & Weston, 2008).

Variable Salaries

If employees must be outsourced during the term of the MES program to conduct specific services for the equipment (external consultants), then their salaries and fees are written as variable expenses (Weaver & Weston, 2008).

Salaries for fixed employees

Wages of permanent employees that operate the equipment are included under the (fixed) salary expense (Weaver & Weston, 2008).

Service and maintenance costs

This is the cost of servicing and performing maintenance on the equipment (Weaver & Weston, 2008). The activities that must be expensed under this category depend on the terms of the MES deal – the extent of maintenance services performed by the MES provider (Costales & Szurovy, 1994) (OEM, 2011).

Insurance

Insurance against theft, accidents, and natural disasters is generally included in an MES program (Weaver & Weston, 2008).

Upgrade costs

Upgrade costs depend on the way the equipment is upgraded as agreed upon in the contract. The cost of new software or hardware for example may be included in the fixed annual fee or the hospital may have to pay it to the MES provider separately. An upgrade may signify complete equipment replacement (Weaver & Weston, 2008).

Rate of inflation

This is especially highly relevant in very long term MES deals (30-40 years). Inflation rate must be included in order to ensure that the supplies recover the value of the medical equipment (Costales & Szurovy, 1994).

The figure in the next page provides a sample cash flow projection for rented or leased equipment flow projections based on both secondary research and interviews with multiple MES providers and MES consultants.

Opening Date	
Cash Balance Minimum	

	P0	P1	P2	P3	P4	P5
Opening Balance						
Cash Inflows						
Project Sales						
Returns						
Collections on accounts receivable						
Interest, other income						
Loan proceeds						
Owner contributions						
Total Cash Receipts						
Total Cash Available						
Cash Outflows						
Commissions and fees						
Salary for variable employees						
Employee benefit programs						
Machine Insurance						
Interest expense						
Materials and supplies (in COGS)						
Administrative Expense						

Selling Expenses						
Rent or lease						
Rent or lease: vehicles, equipment						
Repairs and maintenance						
Taxes and licenses						
Travel						
Salary for fixed employees						
Expense on training of employees						
Miscellaneous expenses						
Subtotal						
Total Cash Paid Out						
Closing Balance						
% Increase		#%	#%	#%	#%	

Table 2: Cash Flow Projection Statement Template (Weaver & Weston, 2008)

Using the next figure, the MES provider can identify when the cash flow has decreased below the specified minimum (e.g. line P6) and following consult with the healthcare provider, and act accordingly.

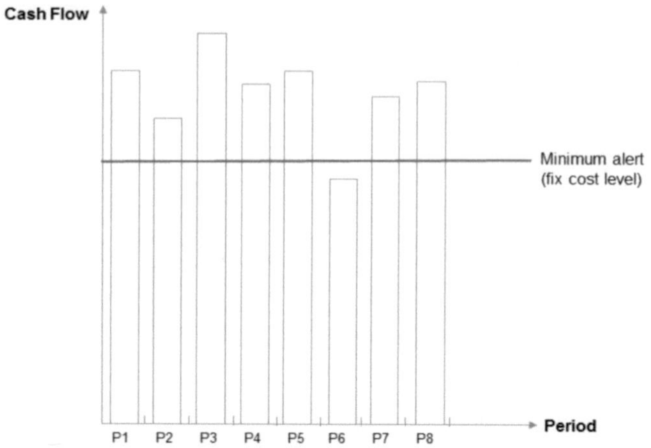

Figure 11: Cash Flow Projection[7]

3.6.2 Pro Forma Income Statement

The pro-forma income statement represents a broad operational plan for the business. It provides income projections for a specific number of years into the future. A pro forma income statement is developed for a specific time in the future using the estimated sales and costs associated with that period (Stevens, Mansfield, Loudon, Wrenn, & Warren, 2006). A sample pro-forma income statement is provided in the next figure.

	P1	**P2**	**P3**	**P4**	**P5**
Revenue					
Sales					
Interest Income					
Other Revenue					
Total Revenue					
Total Cost of Goods Sold					
Gross Profit					

7 Own graph based on analysis of primary and secondary research results.

Operating Expenses					
Training Costs					
Salaries					
Fixed					
Variable					
Service and Maintenance					
Insurance					
Upgrade Costs					
Downtime Penalties					
Inventory Carrying Cost					
Total Operating Expense					
EBIT					
Depreciation					
Interest					
Taxes					
Net Income					

Table 3: Pro Forma Income Statement (Stevens, Mansfield, Loudon, Wrenn, & Warren, 2006)

3.6.3 Project Costing Statement

The project costing template below was developed using activity based costing. Activity based costing uses the concept of assigning costs by the activities performed in the organization. In this method, all costs are collected and summarized for each product/ asset (Kapil, 2011).

Equipment	**X-Ray**	**MR**	**CT**
Quantity			
Onsite Man Needed			
Software Updates Need			
Hardware Update Needed			
Warranty Years			
Total Cost			

Price			
Price / Unit			
Total Price			

Training			
Training Hours/ Machine			
Total Training Hours			
Rate/Hour			
Total Training Cost			
Installation			
Installation Cost/ Machine			
Total Installation Cost			
Human Resources			
Onsite Expert			
Rate per day			
Total Human Resource Cost			
Service			
Servicing Cost/ Machine			
Servicing Required per Year			
Total Service Cost			
Insurance			
Insurance/ Machine			
Total Insurance Cost			
Software Upgrade			
Upgrades Required per Year			
Upgrade Cost/ Machine			
Total Software Upgrade Cost			
Hardware Update			
Upgrades Required per Year			
Upgrade Cost/ Machine			
Total Hardware Upgrade Cost			
Warranty			
Warranty Cost/ Machine			
Total Warranty Cost			
Total Cost			

Table 4: Project Costing Template (Kapil, 2011)

3.7 Total Economic Impact™ Model (TEI)

The Total Economic Impact Methodology was developed by Forrester Research to boost a company's technology decision making process and support vendor, or in this case the MES provider in communicating the value proposition of their products and series. Through the TEI model, the companies can validate, demonstrate, and realize the tangible value of an IT initiative to the management team and to key business stakeholders. While the TEI model has been traditionally employed in the technology and media industries, it has and can be employed in other business schemes. Hence, the TEI model was applied to four variables outlined by Forrester consulting: benefits, costs, risks, and flexibility (Forrester Research Inc., 2009). The TEI model will evaluate the investments made by hospitals based on the benefits, costs, risks, and flexibility of the investment.

3.7.1 Benefits

Forrester consulting defines benefits within the context of the TEI methodology as the value delivered to the user organization by the proposed product project. Benefits, according to Forrester consulting, should be seen beyond IT cost and cost reduction. The focus should rather be placed on the effect that the technology brings on the entire organization. As such within the context of an MES program, benefits represent the value that the services supplied by the MES provider bring to the hospital beyond the value of the added revenue that can be generated from the advanced equipment, cost reductions, and the value of a fixed annual fee. The TEI methodology and the financing model that is generated as a result of the TEI methodology places equal weight on the costs as well as the benefits. This allows a full examination of the effect that an MES program would have on the hospital. In estimating and calculating the value of the benefits, direct dialogue with those that are involved in directly or indirectly using the medical equipment is required. In addition, Forrester also requires that there should be a clear line of accountability established between the measurement and justification of benefit estimates after the project has been completed. Feedback from those who use the equipment provides a clear line of accountability on the weight or placed on the value measured (Weaver & Weston, 2008). This ties the benefit estimate directly back to the bottom line, thereby allowing the MES provider to streamline the service and hospital operations (Forrester Research Inc., 2009).

One of the main benefits of an MES program is that it guarantees equipment uptime by providing engineers who are continuously monitoring, inspecting, and servicing equipment. A benefits model illustrated in Table 5, has been developed in to weigh the value of guaranteed equipment uptime for an MRI machine.

Ref	Metric	Calculation	Per period	Yr 2	Yr3-7	7 year total	PV
B1	Daily revenue from MRI exams						
B2	Average number of days with MRI downtime in a year						
B3	Annual cost of externally servicing equipment						
B4	Annual salaries of medical equipment servicing professional in the hospital						
B5	Total	(B1*B2)-(B3+ B4)					

Table 5: Benefits Calculation of Template (Forrester Research Inc., 2009)

3.7.2 Costs

Within the context of the TEI methodology, costs represent all the investment and expenses required to capture and deliver the value of the benefits in a project. The cost category within TEI captures any incremental costs over the existing environment for ongoing costs associated with the solution. In an MES program, if a new high-tech piece of equipment is to be added, then room renovations/ construction might be required, additional staff must be hired, and additional equipment might be required to operate the new piece of equipment that will be added to the hospital equipment. If a room refurbishment is not included in the contract, then hospital will have to bear the renovation costs as well as the necessary hospital infrastructure upgrades. The following costs have been identified in order to add a new nuclear imaging unit to the hospitals radiology department. The costs identified must be tied to the benefits that are created (Forrester Research Inc., 2009).

- **Infrastructure and equipment cost**

  This is the cost of the necessary infrastructure required to support a nuclear imaging unit (hospital electrical infrastructure upgrade, nuclear safety installations etc). It also includes a cost estimation of the construction contractor hired to build a new room or renovate an existing one if room refurbishment is not a service agreed upon in the MES contract.

- **Labour Cost**

  Labour cost is the cost of the technicians required to operate the nuclear imaging unit.

- **Upgrade cost**

  Upgrade cost is the cost of upgrading the current the equipment and software.

Using the costs identified in the list above, Table 6 provides a sample of a cost calculation template.

Ref	Item	Calculation	Year 1	Year 2	Year 3-7	7-year total	PV
C1	Hospital Infrastructure costs						
C2	Labour and Operating Cost						
C3	Upgrade Cost						
C4	Additional Equipment costs						
C5	Total	∑C1-C4					

Table 6: TEI Cost Calculation Template (Forrester Research Inc., 2009)

3.7.3 Risk

Risk in the TEI methodology is used to measure the uncertainty of the benefit and cost estimates. The likelihood that the cost and benefit estimate will meet the initial investment, and the likelihood that the estimates will be measured and tracked over time are calculated to measure uncertainty. TEI applies a probability density function known as "triangular distribution" to the values entered. (Forrester Research Inc., 2009) A minimum of three values are calculated to estimate the range of each cost and benefit (Forrester Research Inc., 2009). Risk evaluation is a very subjective procedure that is largely dependent on how conservative the person is when evaluating risk. The calculation will also vary depending on the factors that may or may not be measured.

The cost of labor may vary over the years depending on changes in economic and other macroeconomic factors i.e. labor supply vs. demand, minimum wage etc. Thus, the probability of variability must be factored. In calculating risk, Forrester applies the probability density function of triangular distribution; a scale consisting of a minimum of the three probabilities or distributions, must be calculated for each cost and each benefit. When evaluating the U.S market, Forrester uses a risk factor of 110% on the high end of the scale, 108% as the average or medium of the scale, and 100% as the low end of the range to calculate cost. Taking into consideration all of the relevant macroeconomic factors, these probabilities can be adapted to Abu Dhabi's market. The original cost estimate must be revised and increased due to the skewed distribution of the scale used in the U.S market. To avoid over/ undervaluing the risk, the average of the three probabilities is also taken and used in the calculating the costs and benefits of a project (MES program). A sample of how a risk is calculated under the TEI methodology is provided in the table below.

	Component	**Low %**	**Medium %**	**High %**	**Average %**
D1	Labor Cost				
D2	Annual Maintenance Fee				
D3	Reduced Head Count				

Table 7: TEI Risk Assessment Template (Forrester Research Inc., 2009)

3.7.4 Flexibility

Flexibility, as defined by Forrester's TEI methodology (described in more detail in Appendix A), is the term used to indicate an investment in additional capacity or capability that can be turned into future business benefits at some additional cost. This in turn provides the hospital with the "right" or the ability to engage in future initiatives but not the obligation to do so. Therefore, an investment in a technology upgrade can increase productivity (higher patient turnover) and increase process standardization, or reduce the probability of a misdiagnosis due to human error (Forrester Research Inc., 2009).

Using the information generated from the risk, cost, and benefit calculation, the net present value, payback period, and return on investment of both total risk adjusted and risk unadjusted benefits and costs can be calculated. These results could then be used to demonstrate, justify, and realize the tangible value of an MES program to both hospital management and other governmental and nongovernmental stakeholders (Forrester Research Inc., 2009).

Ref	**Total benefits**	**Calculation**	**Risk Adjusted**	**Risk Unadjusted**
R1	Total costs (PV)			
R2	Total benefits (PV)			
R3	Total	R2-R1		
Return on investment		R3/ R1		

Table 8: TEI Composite Risk Adjusted ROI (Forrester Research Inc., 2009)

As demonstrated in the table above, the TEI model is a good tool for both MES providers and healthcare providers to assess not only the profitability of an MES program but also of other less tangible advantages.

4. Overview of the Gulf Cooperation Council

In order to understand the viability of the models developed and MES approach previously discussed, the GCC is chosen as an example. The following insights are therefore the base to understand a theoretical implementation of MES.

The Gulf Region is made up of countries found in the Arabian Peninsula. Covering approximately 3 million square kilometres, the Arabian Peninsula is located in the South-western region of the Asian continent. The Arab states of the Persian Gulf consist of Iraq, the Kingdoms of Bahrain and Saudi Arabia, the Sultanate of Oman, the States of Kuwait and Qatar, and the United Arab Emirates. The last six countries are the members of the Gulf Cooperation Council (GCC).

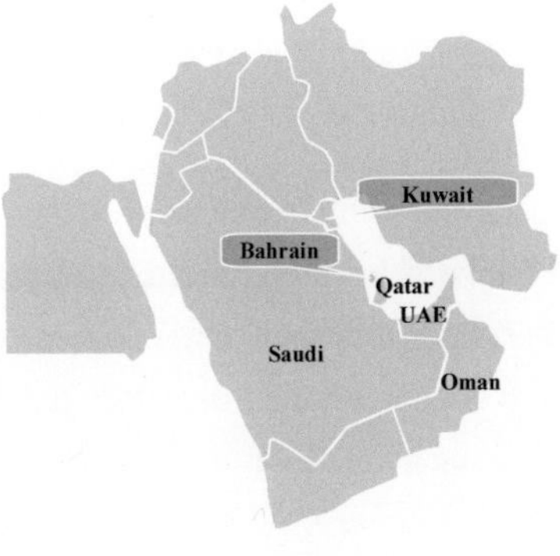

Figure 12: Map of the Gulf Region and GCC Countries

4.1 The Gulf Cooperation Council (GCC)

Gulf Cooperation Council for the Arab States of the Gulf (CCASG) is a trade bloc made up of six Arab States that are located along the Arabian Gulf. GCC was formed in 1981 in the Saudi capital of Riyadh (Encyclopædia Britannica, 2011). The bloc was formed based on similar political systems, Islamic beliefs, joint destiny, and common objectives. The geographic environment of these countries and their implementation of free-trade economic policies were also factors that further encouraged them to establish the GCC (Global Security, 2011). Although both

Iran and Iraq have their shores on the Persian Gulf, they are not members of the GCC as they lack some of the properties held by the other six members, such as their common political system (Rourke, 2008). Throughout history, it has been proven that GCC countries do have some major differences in their "state-religion" relations. Although KSA and Qatar follow the same two Islamic branches, the 'Wahhabi'[8] and the 'Hanbali'[9], they actually go in opposite directions when it comes to internal policies in correspondence to religion (Baskan & Wright, 2011)

On January 1, 2008, a common market for GCC was launched that grants national treatment to all GCC firms and citizens, along with treaties with the EU and the US (Boughanmi, 2008). In doing so the GCC has removed most barriers to trade with investments and services across the countries (Encyclopædia Britannica, 2011). GCC military consists of one infantry brigade; GCC however, cooperates closely with USA to ensure the national security of its six members (Blanche, 2001).

The creation of a monetary union has been the primary objective of the GCC member states since the early 1980s. Members, however, disagree on the exchange-rate regime to be adopted for the single currency. GCC countries peg their currencies to the US dollar as an external anchor for their monetary policy. Nevertheless, recently most of the GCC states have been discussing the possibility of shifting to other currencies, especially with other economic tycoons such as India and China leading the way (Smith P. A., 2009, pp. 55-59). This is partly due to the current economic situation, and imported inflation caused by the dollar (Khan, 2009).

The objectives of GCC are (Hashem, 2007):

- Formulating similar regulations in various fields such as economy, finance, trade, customs, tourism, legislation, and administration

8 Is a school of thought (law) within Sunna that is well known to deterge Islam from its impurities, it was established by Muhammad Ibn Abd al-Wahhab in the 18th century (Klass & Goss, 2003).

9 Is a school of thought (law) within Sunna that heavily depends on Hadith. It was established by Ahmed Ibn Hanbal (a famous Islamic scholar) in d. 855 (Shah, Dayeh, Blatherwick, & Sakaedani, 2007).

- Fostering scientific and technical progress in industry, mining, agriculture, water and animal resources
- Establishing scientific research centres
- Setting up joint ventures
- Encouraging cooperation in the private sector

The following table provides a comparative overview of the profiles of countries in GCC. Each GCC country will be described individually in the rest of this section.

Country	Government	Area (km^2)	Population (2010) (World dataBank, 2011)	Industries
KSA	Monarchy	2,149,690	25,988,900	Petroleum refining, basic petrochemicals, ammonia, industrial gases, sodium hydroxide, cement, fertilizer, plastics, metals, commercial ship repair, commercial aircraft repair, construction, crude oil production
UAE	Federation	83,600	4,707,307	Petroleum and petrochemicals, fishing, aluminium, cement, fertilizers, commercial ship repair, construction materials, boat building, handcrafts, textiles
Kuwait	Constitutional emirate	17,818	2,863,000	Petroleum, petrochemicals, cement, shipbuilding and repair, water desalination, food processing, construction materials
Qatar	Emirate	11,586	1,508,322	Liquefied natural gas, crude oil production and refining, ammonia, fertilizers, petrochemicals, steel reinforcing bars, ce-

				ment, commercial ship repair
Oman	Sultanate	212,457	2,905,114	Liquefied natural gas (LNG), petroleum products, fertilizers, steel
Bahrain	Constitu-tional mon-archy	760	807,131	Petroleum processing and re-fining, aluminium smelting, iron pelletization, fertilizers, Islamic and offshore banking, insurance, ship repairing, tour-ism

Table 9: GCC Country Profiles (CIA, 2011)

4.1.1 Kingdom of Saudi Arabia

Kingdom of Saudi Arabia (KSA) is a monarchy ruled by the Al Saud family. It was founded in 1932 by Abd Al-Azziz bin Abd al-Rahman Al Saud (Ibn Saud) as a result of a 30-year campaign aimed at unifying most of the Arabian Peninsula (CIA, 2011). A written constitution and a bill of rights were introduced during the reign of King Fahd bin Abdul'Aziz Al Saud (1982-2005) (Encyclopædia Britannica, 2011). Following the death of King Fahad bin Abdul Aziz Al Saud, Saudi Arabia has been ruled by King Abdullah bin Abdul Aziz Al Saud. The king of Saudi Arabia also holds the title of Custodian of the Two Holy Mosques.

Saudi Arabia is the birthplace of Islam, and home to the two holy cities of Mecca and Medina. Occupying four-fifths of the Arabian Peninsula (an area of about 2,240,000 square kilometres), KSA is the largest country in the Gulf Region. The Red Sea and the Gulf of Aqaba form KSA's western border; the Republic of Yemen and the Sultanate of Oman form its southern border; the Arabian Gulf, the United Arab Emirates and Qatar form its eastern border;, and Jordan, Iraq, and Kuwait form its northern border. Located in the centre of the country, Riyadh is the Kingdom's capital as well as its largest city. With a border in the Red Sea, Jeddah is the Kingdom's second largest city and the main port through which pilgrims enter to embark on the Umrah and Haj pilgrimages. The richest oil fields in the county are found in the eastern region of the Kingdom (CIA, 2011).

The most important industry in Saudi Arabia is the petroleum and gas industry. The Kingdom has the world's largest proven oil reserves, and is the largest oil producer in the Organization of the Petroleum Exporting Countries (OPEC). "OPEC's objective is to co-ordinate and unify petroleum policies among member countries, in order to secure fair and stable prices for petroleum producers." In diversifying its economy, the Kingdom is promoting heavy industry, such as petrochemicals, fertilizers, and steel. Traditionally, fishing and agriculture were sources of revenue for the Kingdom (Encyclopædia Britannica, 2011).

4.1.2 United Arab Emirates

The UAE was founded by the late Sheikh Zayed bin Sultan Al Nahyan in 1971. The current UAE President, and ruler of the Emirate of Abu Dhabi, is Sheikh Khalifa Bin Zayed Al Nahyan. The Vice President of the UAE and ruler of the emirate of Dubai is Sheikh Mohammed bin Rashid Al Maktoum (CIA, 2011).

The United Arab Emirates (UAE) is a federation of the seven emirates: Abu Dhabi, Dubai, Sharjah, Ajman, Umm Al Qaiwain, Ras Al Khaimah and Fujairah. The UAE covers an area of 83,000 square kilometers, and is located in the South-eastern corner of the Arabian Peninsula, bordered by the Sultanate of Oman to the East, Kingdom of Saudi Arabia to the South and West, and by the Arabian Gulf to the North (Division, Federal Research, 2007).

In 2009, the total population of the UAE was estimated to be 5.4 million with growing at a rate of 4.7% CAGR (Division, Federal Research, 2007). The population of UAE is composed of predominantly expatriates; these expatriates constitute 88% of the population (Encyclopædia Britannica, 2011). UAE has the highest population count as well as the highest growth rate among GCC countries. As based on the World Population Prospects 2010 Revision, a breakdown of the population by age group and gender based on the World Population Prospects 2010 Revision, has been provided in the next table.

Age Structure	Both Sexes	Male	Female
0-4	421	216	205
5-9	411	214	197
10-14	448	236	212
15-19	429	224	205
20-24	782	497	285
25-29	1,240	908	332
30-34	1,231	951	279
35-39	967	750	217
40-44	667	520	147
45-49	435	337	98
50-54	272	212	59
55-59	131	101	31
60-64	47	37	10
65-69	13	10	3
70-74	9	5	3
75-79	5	3	2
80-84	3	1	1
85-89	2	1	1
90-94	1	0	0
95-99	0	0	0
100+	0	0	0

Table 10: UAE Population by Age-Group and Gender in Thousands, 2010 (Population Division, DESA, 2011)

When calculating patient load in a hospital, the population age structure must be considered as it correlates with the incidence of disease rates. Majority of UAE's population is made up of expatriate males between 20 to 50 years of age; this large group is mainly composed of the foreign manual labour (Encyclopædia Britannica, 2011).

In the UAE, the life expectancy at birth has been gradually improving over the years. According to the CIA World Fact Book, in 1970, UNICEF reported a life expectancy of 61 years for the region. In 2002, the life expectancy was 72.5 years (71.3 years for males and 75.1 years for females) and in 2009, the life expectancy rose to 76.11 years (73.56 years male and 78.78 years female).

This increase in life expectancy at birth, reflects an improvement in the region's health status. Improvements in healthcare, hygiene, nutrition, and preventive measures taken by the government and the communities had a positive effect on the country's health profile. Life expectancy at birth in UAE is among the highest. Compared to other neighbouring countries, the UAE has the lowest death rate (CIA, 2011).

4.1.3 Kuwait

Kuwait is a constitutional monarchy governed by the Al Sabah family, the ruling family since 1756. (Ahmed Al Jaber Al Sabah is the current Emir of Kuwait). Britain oversaw foreign relations and defence for the ruling Kuwaiti Al-Sabah dynasty from 1899, until its independence in 1961 (Encyclopædia Britannica, 2011). Kuwait is located in the North-eastern corner of the Arabian Peninsula. It is bordered by Iraq in the North and Northwest, by Saudi Arabia in the South and Southwest, and by the Arabian Gulf to the East. Kuwait covers an area of approximately 17,818 square kilometres which includes nine Gulf islands on the gulf. Kuwait was attacked and overrun by Iraq on 2 August 2, 1990. Following several weeks of aerial bombardment, a US-led, UN coalition began a ground assault on 23 February 23, 1991 that liberated Kuwait in four days (CIA, 2011).

Crude oil and refined products account for most of the country's exports. Kuwait's reserves of crude oil have been estimated to amount to 10% of the world total oil reserves; the third largest oil reserve in the world (CIA, 2011). The capital Kuwait City is an important port for oil, and the production of petroleum products. The city of Al Jahrah is the centre of the country's agricultural industry, which primarily produces fruit and vegetables (CIA, 2011).

4.1.4 Qatar

Ruled by the Al-Thani family since the mid-1800s, Qatar transformed itself from a poor British protectorate noted mainly for its pearling industry, into an independent state with significant oil and natural gas revenues. Sheikh Hamad bin Khalifa Al Thani has been Emir (Prince) since early 1995 (CIA, 2011). Sheikh Abdullah bin Khalifah Al Thani is the prime minister. Qatar is a peninsula, which extends northward for about 180 kilometres into the Arabian Gulf. The country is bordered to the South by Saudi Arabia for a stretch of 56 kilometres. The total area of Qatar is 11,437 square kilometres. The capital of the Qatar is Doha, located on the East coast (Encyclopædia Britannica, 2011).

Qatar produces less than 1% of the world's oil output. Crude oil and liquefied natural gas account for about 80% of the country's exports. The banking sector also plays an important role in Qatar's economy (Encyclopædia Britannica, 2011). In 1990 the world's largest gas field was developed in the northern part of the country. Since then, Qatar has been among the countries with the highest per-capita income in the world (CIA, 2011).

4.1.5 Oman

Sultanate of Oman is ruled by Al Said Dynasty. Sultan Qaboos bin Said Al Said has ruled since 1970. The Sultan also holds the posts of Prime Minister, Minister of Defence, Minister of Foreign Affairs, and Minister of Finance. Prior to this, the country was known as Muscat and Oman until the Al Said family started ruling it in 1744 (CIA, 2011).

Muscat has been the capital of Oman since 1741. Oman covers an area of about 212,457 squared kilometres along the South-eastern coast of the Arabian Peninsula. Yemen forms Oman's South-western border, Saudi Arabia forms its western border, the United Arab Emirates forms its North-western border, the Gulf of Oman forms its northern border, and the Arabian Sea forms its eastern and southern border. Oman also borders the Strait of Hormuz, which is a waterway linking the Gulf of Oman to the Arabian Gulf. Due to its strategic location at the mouth of the Gulf, the country is considered an important trade port (CIA, 2011).

Early in the 1900s, Oman mainly depended on fishing, foreign trading, and agriculture (Encyclopædia Britannica, 2011). Later Oman's primary resources became petroleum and natural gas. Its petroleum reserves are not substantial, and therefore, the government is working on transforming Oman into a major natural-gas exporter (CIA, 2011).

4.1.6 Bahrain

Bahrain is an independent state with a traditional monarchy. Bahrain is ruled by Al Khalifa family who captured it from the Persians in 1783. The country entered into a series of treaties with the UK during the 19th century through which it became a British protectorate. Bahrain however attained its independence in 1971, and in 2002, it was declared a Kingdom. Sheikh Hamad bin Isa Al Khalifa is the King, and has ruled Bahrain since 1999. Sheikh Khalifa bin Salman Al Khalifa is the Prime Minister (Encyclopædia Britannica, 2011).

Bahrain is the largest island in an archipelago of thirty-three islands. Located in the Arabian Gulf, the islands are about twenty-four kilometres from the East coast of Saudi Arabia and twenty-eight kilometres from Qatar. The total area of the islands is about 678 square kilometres. The capital, Manama, is located on the north-eastern tip of the island of Bahrain. Bahrain's international airport is located in Al Muharraq; the second largest island which is also linked by a causeway to KSA (Encyclopædia Britannica, 2011).

Oil was discovered in commercial quantities in Bahrain in 1932. In comparison to the other Gulf States, Bahrain's oil reserves are small. Facing declining oil reserves, the country has resorted to petroleum processing and refinement to renew the health of its economy. It has also transformed itself into an international banking centre. (CIA, 2011)

4.2 Economics of the GCC

The key factors that have a direct effect on the healthcare industry are identified and described in this section. The six factors are Gross Domestic Product (GDP), inflation rate, unemployment rate, growth rate, quality of life, and the level of Foreign Direct Investment (FDI).

4.2.1 Gross Domestic Product (GDP)

With regards to the level of investment on developing healthcare, GDP can be used to estimate the purchasing power of each the GCC country. Even though most of the GCC countries have been heavily dependent on expatriate labour force, due to the relatively rapid economic growth, Saudi Arabia and Oman are not following the same pattern. In 1997, for instance, the expatriate labour force in KSA and Oman constitutes 64% and 55% of the entire labour force, respectively (Harb, 2009). However, these percentages have almost doubled over the next ten years. A large majority of the GCC states' GDP is attributed to oil and petroleum Oil Export Revenues (OER) (Harb, 2009). Saudi Arabia is GCC's largest oil producer, generating 8.146 billion barrels of oil (Harb, 2009). This amount accounts for approximately 45% of KSA's US$369.2 billion GDP, the 23rd highest GDP in the world and the highest amongst the GCC states (CIA, 2011). (CIA, 2011). KSA's GDP per capita however is the lowest amongst the GCC members, valued at US$14,450.0 in 2009 (CIA, 2011).

Among the GCC countries, UAE has the second highest GDP, valued at US$224.9 billion in 2009. The UAE has made substantial efforts to diversify its economy, and as such, it is not as oil-dependent as its neighbour Saudi Arabia (Harb, 2009). UAE GDP per capita in 2009 is valued at US$41,390, the 19th highest GDP in the world. With a US$145.7 billion GDP, Kuwait has the 3rd highest GDP among GCC countries (CIA, 2011). This figure is relatively high and is attributed to the fact that Kuwait holds 9% of the world's oil reserves. Due to Kuwait's small population size and its high GDP, its GDP per capita is US$54,100, the 7th highest GDP in the world (Encyclopædia Britannica, 2011).

Due to similar economic diversification efforts, Qatar's GDP has reached US$101.4 billion in 2009. With US$121,700 GDP per capita in 2009, Qatar has the second highest GDP in the world (Encyclopædia Britannica, 2011). Oman, due to increasing tourism investments, has increased its GDP to US$69.48 billion. Valued at US$23,900, Oman's GDP per capita is similar to that of Saudi Arabia's; however, that can of course be contributed to their population differences. Bahrain's economy is not as diversified as that of the United Arab Emirates and Qatar; it relies heavily on oil revenues and has a GDP of US$27.99 billion. Bahrain's GDP per capita has been valued at US$38,500, the 25th highest GDP per capita in the world (CIA, 2011).

Such economic diversification efforts are in fact on par with some of the latest work done on the region in the literature. In Harb's "Oil Exports, Non-Oil GDP, and Investment in the GCC Countries" (2009) show that there is a rather weak correlation between OER and Non-Oil GDP (NGDP). Given his conclusion, this shows that NGDP, including healthcare, do not necessarily have a cause-and-effect relationship.

4.2.2 Inflation Rate

Analyzing inflation rate is pertinent for the purpose of this analysis, as the depreciation of GCC currencies might cause healthcare investments to become more expensive for the GCC states. The GCC states generally import all their medical equipment from foreign companies which might be paid in their associated local currencies (Thompson, 2009). Therefore, it would cost more for a specific GCC currency to purchase a piece of medical equipment that is priced in Euros or US dollars.

The GCC countries have suffered from relatively high inflation rates since 2003. This could be attributed to the fact that all the GCC countries peg their currencies to the U.S. dollar. Due to the U.S. dollar depreciation against most major currencies, GCC countries suffer from imported inflation (Morsy & Kandil, 2009). In addition, major GCC foreign traders have suffered from inflation due to their flourishing OER (Harb, 2009). Increasing OER has drastically increased credit investments and aggregate spending in general, worsening the existing inflation problems. The country with the highest inflation rate (5.7% in 2010) in GCC is Saudi Arabia (CIA, 2011). Saudi Arabia's inflation rate would have been greater, if Saudi Arabian Monetary Agency (SAMA) hadn't taken measures to prevent further inflation such as increases in commercial bank reserve requirements (Morsy & Kandil, 2009).

Following Saudi Arabia, the countries with the highest inflation rates are Oman (4%), Kuwait (3.8% in 2010), Bahrain (3.3% in 2010), UAE (2.2% in 2010), Qatar (1.1% in 2010) (CIA, 2011).

4.2.3 Unemployment Rate

A common trend among all the GCC countries is that the majority of the labour force is made up of expatriates. As such, the size of the labour force of each GCC country was measured. The size of each of the GCC country's labour force and the percentage of expatriates are described below:

- Saudi Arabia's labour force is made up of 6.992 million people, 64% of whom are non-nationals (Karoly, 2010).
- United Arab Emirates' labour force is made of 3.152 million people, 85% of whom are non-nationals (Roubini Global Economics, 2011).
- The Kuwait labour force is made up of 2.04 million people, 80% of whom are expatriates (Chemingui, 2008).
- Qatar's labour force is made up of 1.179 million people, 52% of whom are non-nationals (Karoly, 2010).
- Oman's labour force is made up of 968,000 people, 60% of whom are non-nationals (CIA, 2011).
- Bahrain's labour force is estimated at 595,000 and 44% of the population within the age group of 15-64 is made up of expatriates (CIA, 2011).

Due to the rapid growth rate the GCC economies have experienced recently after the discovery of oil, these countries needed to support their large economies by importing labour forces for most of their major activities. As a result, expatriates makeup 42% of the region's population (Kinninmont, 2009). According to the Episcom Intelligence report, *GCC in 2020: The Gulf and its People*, "The rising expatriate population will contribute to economic growth. An expanding pool of skilled professionals from overseas will provide a diverse talent pool, which should help to stimulate further economic diversification" (Kinninmont, 2009)

Unemployment rates and figures in the GCC are not considered reliable due to the questionable methods used to gather data, as well as the quality of the data being gathered. According to the CIA World Fact Book, Kuwait and Oman last recorded their unemployment rate in the year 2004 (CIA, 2011). Bahrain last recorded its unemployment rate in 2005. In addition, some GCC countries such as Saudi Arabia only measure the unemployment of males and not females (Office of the Chief Economist, 2010). Unemployment has been a persistent issue in the GCC, especially in the KSA. Privately calculated estimates, often more reliable than government estimates especially in the MENA region, show that Saudi Arabia has almost 25-30% unemployment rate (Maben, Al-Thowini, West, & Rafferty, 2009). This has lead GCC governments to put countless efforts and dedicate a considerable amount of their investments to address and solve these issues. Official reports show that Saudi Arabia's unemployment rate is estimated to be 10.8% as of 2010, the highest unemployment rate compared to other GCC countries. This rate could be assumed to be higher, as it is only a measure of the unemployment rate among males who constitute around half of Saudi Arabia's population (CIA, 2011). Not to mention, such figures cannot be compared to other GCC countries given the data credibility issue discussed earlier.

Oman and Bahrain have both recorded an unemployment rate of 15%, these countries however have not recorded their unemployment rates since 2005 (CIA, 2011). In 2004, Kuwait had an unemployment rate of 2.2% (CIA, 2011). United Arab Emirates last recorded its unemployment of 2.4% rate in 2001, the 20th lowest unemployment rate in the world (CIA, 2011). The GCC country with the lowest unemployment rate is Qatar, with 0.5% in unemployment according to 2010 estimates. This is the second lowest unemployment rate in the world, following Monaco that has recorded a 0% unemployment rate (CIA, 2011). This again raises the data credibility issue as it is reported in a RAND report that Qatar has a 2.4% unemployment rate (Karoly, 2010).

4.2.4 Real Growth Rate

Rapid growth rates indicate investments in infrastructure and economic diversification. The GCC countries have attractive real growth rates which could be used to indicate how well prepared they are to launch new healthcare projects. Due to massive internal investments, the UAE has grown at a very rapid rate. In 2010, while the UAE suffered from a negative growth rate in 2009 due to the global economic crisis, its growth rate was estimated at 3.2% (Roubini Global

Economics, 2011). Kuwait's growth rate in 2010 was two percent, which was among the lowest in the GCC. Saudi Arabia has a growth rate of 3.7%. Oman, recorded a growth rate of 4.2%, according to 2010 estimates. Bahrain has a growth rate of 4.1% according to 2010 estimates (CIA, 2011).

Qatar has proved to be one of most attractive economies amongst the GCC states in regards to all of the economic indicators that have been analyzed. Qatar has recorded a real growth rate of 16.3%, the highest growth rate in the world by far (Roubini Global Economics, 2011).

4.2.5 Quality of Life

To measure the overall attractiveness of an economy, International Living's Quality of Life Index can be used. This index measures the quality of life in 194 countries based on nine different criteria. Each criterion is given a score out of 100; the weighted average of each criterion's score is then added to reach the final measure. The nine factors that affect the quality of life are cost of living (20%), leisure and culture (10%), economy (15%), environment (5%), freedom (10%), health (10%), infrastructure (10%), risk and safety (10%), and climate (10%) (Diener & Suh, 1997) (K. Aaronson, et al., 1992).

Cost of living refers to how much it would cost to live abroad; cost of living is evaluated based on information from the U.S. State Department's Index of Overseas Living Costs. Culture and leisure is measured through an evaluation of "Literacy rates, newspaper circulation, primary and secondary school enrollment ratios, number of people per museum, and a subjective rating of the variety of cultural and recreational offerings" (International Living, 2010). The strength of a country's economy is evaluated based on GDP, GDP growth rate, GDP per capita, inflation rate, and GNP per capita. The quality of a country's environment is evaluated based on population density per square kilometer, population growth rate, greenhouse emissions per capita, and the percentage of total land that is protected. The freedom criterion is measured using *Freedom House's* survey; political rights and civil liberty, however are stressed (Diener & Suh, 1997). The health criteria is a composite measure of calorie consumption as a percentage of daily requirements, the number of doctors per thousand, the number of hospital beds per thousand people, the percentage of the population with access to safe water, infant mortality rate, life expectancy, and public health expenditure as a percentage of a country's GDP. Infrastructure is calculated based on the length of railways, paved highways, and navigable waterways in each country in consideration to the country's population and size (K. Aaronson, et al., 1992). The number of airports, motor vehicles, telephones, internet service providers, and cell phones per capita are also incorporated when calculating infrastructure. Risk and safety is measured based on the U.S. Department of State's hardship differentials and danger allowances. Climate favorability is evaluated based on annual rainfall, average temperature, and natural disaster risk considerations. In Table 11 below, the quality of life in each of the GCC countries is measured, and then ranked according the country's overall score compared to other GCC countries (International Living, 2010).

Criteria	KSA	UAE	Kuwait	Qatar	Oman	Bahrain
Cost of Living	67	43	46	59	62	53
Leisure and Culture	68	47	74	66	63	70
Economy	56	58	75	85	65	68
Environment	38	14	31	27	22	16
Freedom	8	25	50	25	25	25
Health	74	76	70	74	73	74
Infrastructure	42	77	46	59	38	86
Risk and Safety	50	93	79	84	82	86
Climate	23	10	18	13	2	30
Final Score	48	50	54	57	51	58
Rank	6	5	3	2	4	1

Table 11: Quality of Life GCC Country Ranking (International Living, 2010)

Bahrain, according to the criteria evaluated, has the highest quality of life. Compared to other GCC countries, Bahrain's scores are especially high in regards to infrastructure as well as in regards to risk and safety. KSA has the lowest quality of life compared to other GCC countries; this is mainly due to very low scores in the freedom, as well as in the risk and safety criteria. Compared to the other 188 countries evaluated, the quality of life provided in GCC countries is considered to be average. The country with the highest score (86) is the United States (International Living, 2010).

4.2.6 Human Development Index (HDI)

The human development index, published by the United Nations Development Program is a composite measure of a country's progress (McGillivray, 1991). The Index is calculated based on three factors: education, health, and income (as a measure of living standards). Accordingly, four indicators are used to measure human development: life expectancy at birth (to evaluate health), the mean number of school years and the expected years of schooling (to evaluate education), and Gross National Income (GNI) per capita (to measure living standards) (Klugman, 2010). Table 12 below identifies each GCC country's score and ranking on the Human Development Index.

Country	GCC HDI Ranking	HDI Value	Life Expectancy at Birth	Mean School Years	Expected Years of Schooling	GNI per Capita (2008)
KSA	5	.752	73.3	7.8	13.5	US$24,726
UAE	1	.815	77.7	9.2	11.5	US$58,006
Kuwait	4	.771	77.9	6.1	12.5	US$55,719
Qatar	2	.803	76.0	7.3	12.7	US$79,426
Oman	-	-	76.1		11.1	US$25,653
Bahrain	3	.801	76.0	9.4	14.3	US$26,664

Table 12: GCC Human Development Index (CIA, 2011)

According to The World Fact Book United Arab Emirates (32nd place), Qatar (38th place), and Bahrain (39th place) are amongst countries with the highest level of human development in the world. Norway has the highest HDI score (.938). With a life expectancy of 81.9 years, Australia has the highest level of development in terms of health and the highest overall HDI score (CIA, 2011). In comparison to other countries, UAE had the second highest score across all categories. With the lowest score across all categories, Saudi Arabia had the lowest level of progress compared to other GCC countries. Progress in terms of health in Saudi Arabia (measured through life expectancy) is much lower than that of other GCC countries; KSA has a life expectancy of 73.3 years; 3 years lower than the average life expectancy in GCC countries (76.1 years). Compared to other GCC countries, Kuwait has the highest level of development in health (Klugman, 2010).

4.2.7 Level of Foreign Direct Investment (FDI)

Upon analyzing the different economies of GCC, one major factor that must be studied is the size of the Foreign Direct Investment (FDI) that is being pumped into each of these economies. This is highly relevant when looking into the healthcare industry due to the high percentage of money being reinvested into infrastructure industries such as the healthcare industry. The GCC can benefit from increasing the FDI by increasing production, the technical knowledge which may also help diversify the economy (Mina, 2007).

Foreign direct investments in GCC are at their highest. Beginning from the 1990s, there has been a high inflow of FDI; during this time GCC countries began to diversify their economies. Between the years 2003 and 2008, GCC countries recorded a 57.2% increase in FDI. In 2009 the level of FDI increased by 31.5% despite the global economic crisis (The Free Library, 2009). In 2010, however, FDI in GCC dropped 15% from its 2009 levels to US$39.9 billion.

Saudi Arabia has the highest FDI among GCC countries; it recorded US$28 billion in FDI in 2010; a 12% drop from the previous year. Between the years 2003-2008, however, Saudi Arabia recorded a 117.9% increase in FDI. However, it dropped in the following year due to the global economic crisis (Kinninmont, 2009).

Qatar has the second highest FDI volume after Saudi Arabia, with US$5.5 billion recorded in 2010. With US$13.7 billion in FDI in 2010, UAE has the third highest FDI volume among GCC countries. Bahrain FDI reached US$1.7 billion with 2.2% of its GDP composed of FDI has the second lowest FDI among GCC countries (Kinninmont, 2009).

In contrast to other GCC countries, Kuwait and Oman have experienced a drop in FDI. The FDI in Oman decreased by 6.3% in 2010 compared to the previous year, while Kuwait recorded 54.5% drop in FDI inflows. Nevertheless, the FDI average for the GCC is still very high (Kinninmont, 2009).

4.2.8 Key Similarities and Trends

After analyzing GCC economies, two major trends were identified that have proven to have a high impact on the healthcare industry in the GCC. The first trend observed is a high dependence on the oil industry and oil sales, which account for a great portion of each GCC country's GDP (Morris, 2009). GCC countries account for almost 40% of the world's oil reserves, which is valued at US$18.3 trillion (Morris, 2009). Pioneered by Saudi Arabia in the 1990s, GCC countries have begun to diversify their economies in order to ensure sustainability. The diversification strategy is relevant, to the scope of this dissertation, as healthcare represents one of the major industries used for economic diversification purposes (Morris, 2009). Billions of dollars are being pumped into implementing different policies aimed at improving healthcare in GCC (Maben, Al-Thowini, West, & Rafferty, 2009).

The second trend observed is that GCC countries are very dependent on FDI inflow. It could be concluded that due to the magnitude of the projects GCC countries are endeavouring in, their federal savings (without substantial FDI) are not adequate to sustain their high growth rates. Therefore, GCC have turned to FDI inflows to continue the momentum that they have attained, and to proceed with the projects planned. Dependence on FDI however has left GCC countries highly vulnerable to global economic downturns. During the global economic crisis, the overall level of FDI has decreased significantly as investors became more risk averse, and thus GCC economies have suffered (Maben, Al-Thowini, West, & Rafferty, 2009).

4.3 Healthcare in the GCC

Due to a combination of steadily increasing crude oil prices and increasing demand from a growing and ageing population, Middle East countries have been highlighted as very attractive markets. According to Frost and Sullivan's report on GCC healthcare published in 2009, UAE's healthcare market is supported by domestic credit expansion, high population growth, infrastructure spending, and its oil sectors. In addition, the UAE's healthcare sector has been privatized in the 1900s which lead to an increase in the number of hospitals and physicians (Encyclopædia Britannica, 2011). Kuwait follows a similar pattern, its healthcare sectors is largely supported by its growing oil sector. Large-scale projects have also been planned for the non-oil sectors, among which is the health sector. Qatar's healthcare market is promoted through its growing oil and non-oil sectors, hydrocarbon boom, which contribute to large external and fiscal surpluses that could be invested in healthcare. Oman and Bahrain both rely heavily on oil to expand their economy; Oman's service sector and its oil and gas based industry are the main drivers of growth. While Bahrain highly depends on its oil sector for support, there is an ongoing diversification plan aimed at financial services manufacturing and tourism (Frost & Sullivan, 2009).

Large scale medical complexes are being built that provide services for substantially lower costs (or no cost at all) than those provided in developed countries. Healthcare in the Arabian Gulf states is dominated by the government. According to Sebastian Miasel and John Shoup in their book *Saudi Arabia and the Gulf Arab States Today: A-J*, "Healthcare is the domain of the government, usually the Ministry of Health which provides preventive, curative, and rehabilitative care through a network of medical institutions such as local healthcare centres, regular hospitals, and specialized clinics" (Maisel & Shoup, 2009, p. 189). In fact, according to Frost and Sullivan, the government accounts for approximately 70% of healthcare projects (Frost & Sullivan, 2009). Healthcare is also provided by other state agencies such as the military (Maisel & Shoup, 2009).

Currently there is a regional concentration of healthcare services, with most healthcare services located in the major cities (Frost & Sullivan, 2009).

Healthcare costs however are expected to increase, and such GCC governments are promoting the growth of the private healthcare sector; according to Alpen Capital, "Qatar, Bahrain, and the UAE have been most proactive [...] by providing concrete incentives to attract private investment, including commitments to reimburse a minimum number of patient visits to such hospitals, even if the number of patients is less" (Alpen Capital Limited, 2009, S. 5). A minimum of 200 to 250 new healthcare facilities will be developed on a Greenfield basis in KSA, UAE, and Turkey in the next five years (ATKearney, 2008). GCC governments are promoting private participation by recruiting private players in the healthcare industry to manage public hospitals. This has led to the growth of public private partnerships in the healthcare industry through projects such as the Cleveland Clinic in Abu Dhabi, and Tawam hospital (Alpen Capital Limited, 2009) (Mubadala, 2010). Cleveland Clinic in Abu Dhabi is a hospital built on a partnership between government-owned Mubadala Healthcare, (a division of Mubadala Development Company) and the Cleveland Clinic; the Cleveland Clinic will be in charge of operating the hospital.

It has been predicted that the healthcare industry in GCC will grow to reach US$55 billion by 2020; this is equivalent to a 9% Compound Annual Growth Rate (CAGR) (Zawya, 2009) (Rahman, 2009). The healthcare sector in GCC countries is expected to grow at a rate that is sustainable (Sambidge, 2010). Demand for healthcare in the GCC is expected to increase due to demographic factors such as an increase in the size of aging population (due to an increase in life expectancy healthcare services) that have a higher demand for healthcare services. A surge in the overall size of the population due to the high inflow of expatriates and due to increasing birth rates is also expected to increase the demand for healthcare services (Kinninmont, 2009). High demand for healthcare creates vast opportunities for investment in the healthcare market. In addition, an increase in lifestyle diseases such as obesity and obesity related complications (diabetes and cardiovascular disease) is likely to increase demand for associated specialized healthcare services. A shift towards mandatory health insurance is also likely to cause a boost in healthcare expenditures (Alpen Capital Limited, 2009).

The rest of this section covers healthcare expenditure, public private partnerships, the free healthcare system, health insurance, and new healthcare projects in GCC. Key challenges facing the healthcare sector will also be assessed.

4.3.1 Expenditures on Healthcare in the GCC

The countries that are expected to drive global growth in the healthcare sector are Saudi Arabia, UAE, Turkey, Poland, Russia, China, India, Brazil, and Mexico. Overall, GCC countries are experiencing prominent growth in the healthcare sector (ATKearney, 2008). Overall healthcare expenditures in the GCC are expected to reach a total of US$60 billion in 2025 (Mourshed, Hediger, & Lambert, Gulf Cooperation Council Health Care: Challenges and Opportunities, 2007). (Mourshed, Hediger, & Lambert, 2007) UAE and Saudi Arabia dominate the healthcare industry in the Arabian Gulf region in terms of overall value. As such expenditures in Saudi Arabia will be explored in more depth. As this analysis focuses on UAE, the details of UAE health expenditure are thoroughly covered in the 4th section of the report, and therefore are briefly mentioned in this chapter. The latest figures that are publicly published have been reviewed for each country, and as such different time frames are given.

Healthcare treatment demand is expected to increase by 240% within the next two decades (Mourshed, Hediger, & Lambert, 2007). Three corresponding trends in the GCC have led to the development of the healthcare market in GCC countries:

- Increasing affluence in the region driven by elevated oil prices has led to an increase in demand for high-scale medical facilities.
- An increase in chronic diseases such as high blood pressure has in turn led to an increase in long-term treatment costs.
- The high number of expatriates required to support GCC economies has also led to an increase in demand for premium medical facilities.

UAE's and Bahrain's healthcare sectors are expected to have the highest compound annual growth rates (CAGRs) (Business Monitor International, 2010). In order to evaluate the size of the healthcare market in the GCC, this section will provide information on the size of the expenditures invested by each GCC country. The next graph provides a comparison of the size of the healthcare expenditures spent by each GCC country in relation to the expenditures spent by U.S and Germany as of 2009.

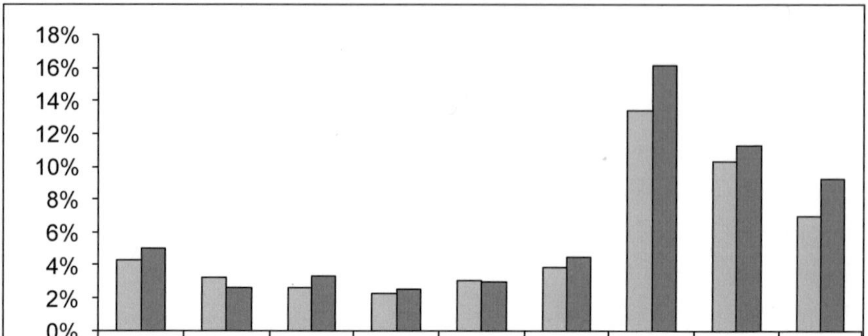

	K.S.A.	U.A.E.	Kuwait	Qatar	Oman	Bahrain	U.S.	Germany	U.K.
2000	4,3%	3,2%	2,6%	2,3%	3,1%	3,9%	13,4%	10,3%	7,0%
2009	5,0%	2,6%	3,3%	2,5%	3,0%	4,5%	16,2%	11,3%	9,3%

Figure 13: GCC and Developed Countries Health Expenditure as a Percent of GDP (WHOSIS, 2010)

The following table lists each GCC country's current or forecasted expenditures in healthcare. The size of the financial investments in healthcare in the next table and the forecasted expenditures required in previous graph both demonstrate the willingness of GCC states, as well as their need to invest substantial sums of money for the development of their healthcare sectors.

Gulf State	Healthcare Expenditure
Kingdom of Saudi Arabia	US$17.7 billion
Bahrain	US$329.7 million
United Arab Emirates	US$5.8 billion
Qatar	Not published
Oman	US$1.2 billion
Kuwait	Not published

Table 13: Healthcare Expenditure Volume in GCC by Country in 2009 (Global Health Expenditure Database, 2009)

A) Saudi Arabia

A large sum of money was invested into the healthcare industry; in 2009; overall healthcare expenditure in the Kingdom in 2009 was US$17.7 billion (4.8% of GDP). This amounts to US$693.7 per capita (Espicom Business Intelligence, 2010). Saudi Arabia allocated US$61.2 billion for building 92 new hospitals with an aggregate of 17,150 beds. The new healthcare facilities planned for development in the region will lead to the recruitment of expatriate healthcare professionals as well as to an increase in demand for medical equipment and supplies (Espicom Business Intelligence, 2009).

The public healthcare sector dominates Saudi Arabia's healthcare market; public healthcare expenditures represent 75% of total healthcare expenditures in the country. Saudi Arabia's immense oil and natural gas reserves relatively ensure a stable economy that has facilitated the development of a sophisticated healthcare system (K. Aaronson, et al., 1992). The country heavily invests in healthcare infrastructure development. In 2009, 23.2% (U.S. 13.9 billion) of the government's budget was allocated to the health and social affairs budget (U.S.-Saudi Arabian Business Council, 2010). In 2010, Saudi Arabia allocated US$16.3 billion to its health and social affairs budget. A large percentage of this budget will be allocated towards modernizing the countries healthcare system. According to the U.S. Arabian Business Council, "The government has allocated funds to the construction of 92 new hospitals, with a capacity of 17,150 beds, along with a number of primary health care facilities. In addition, the government has budgeted for the establishment of a number of sports clubs and sports cities to promote healthy lifestyles" (U.S.-Saudi Arabian Business Council, 2010, p. 1). The next table specifies and forecasts Saudi Arabia's key healthcare indicators from 2008 to 2013.

	2008	2009	2010	2011	2012	2013
Medical Device Market (US$ millions)	781	847	921	1,001	1,090	1,196
Per Capita (US$)	31	33	35	37	39	42
As % of Health Expenditure	4.0	5.3	5.1	4.9	5.0	4.4
Population (millions)*	25.0	25.8	26.6	27.4	28.2	29.0

Growth (%)*	3.0	3.0	3.0	3.0	3.0	3.0
Number Age 65+ (millions) *	0.6	0.6	0.6	0.7	0.7	0.7
Age 65+ (%)*	2.4	2.4	2.4	2.5	2.5	2.6
Hospital Beds (000s)	57.5	59.3	61.2	63.0	64.9	66.7
Private (%)	23.0	23.0	23.0	23.0	23.0	23.0
Rate/ 000	2.3	2.3	2.3	2.3	2.3	2.3
Physicians (000s)	47.5	54.0	55.9	57.5	59.2	60.9
Private (%)	30.9	30.9	30.9	30.9	30.9	30.9
Rate/ 000	1.9	2.1	2.1	2.1	2.1	2.1
GDP (US$ billions)*	467.1	330.7	392.4	423.8	454.2	465.8
GDP Per Capita (US$)*	18,670	12,910	14,940	15,740	16,460	16,470
Real Growth (%)*	4.2	0.4	3.3	3.7	4.0	3.9
Source: KSA Department of Health, *Economist Intelligence Unit (EIU), Espicom estimates.						

Table 14: Saudi Arabia- Key Health Indicators 2008-2013[10]

In 2008 the medical equipment market in Saudi Arabia has been estimated to be worth US$781 million. The value of the equipment market per capita (US$33 per capita) in Saudi Arabia is much lower than what is to be expected for a market its size. Saudi Arabia's medical equipment market is expected to grow by 7% CAGR from SR 1.8 billion (US$479 million) in 2008 to SR2.5 billion (US$672 million) in 2013. In addition, the healthcare market in Saudi Arabia is expected to grow at a very high rate (8.7% per year) due to investments in infrastructure and manpower development, and due to growth in the private sector. In 2013 the medical equipment market has been forecasted to be worth US$1.2 billion, or US$42 per capita. (International Living, 2010) (Espicom Business Intelligence, 2009)

[10] Based on source: Espicom Saudi Arabia Medistat Outlook QII 2009. Latest reports might differ.

In particular, diagnostic imaging will increase from US$171 million in 2008 to US$250 million in 2013 (Espicom Business Intelligence, 2009). The next graph provides a forecast for the value of diagnostic imaging equipment from 2008 to 2013.

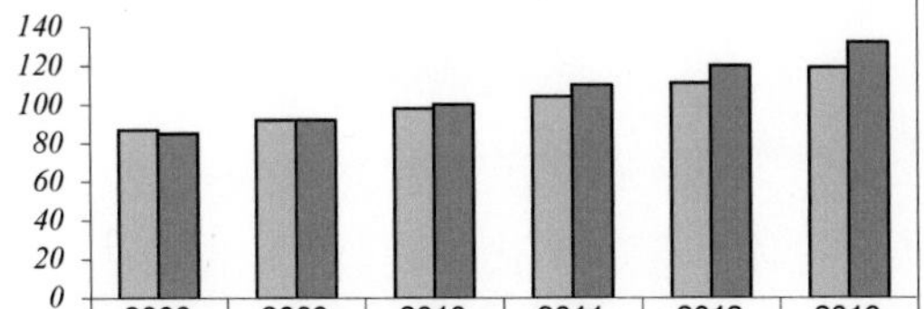

	2008	2009	2010	2011	2012	2013
Electrodiagnostic	87	92	98	104	111	119
X-ray apparatus	85	92	100	110	120	132

Figure 14: Saudi Arabia's Electro-diagnostic and X-ray Apparatus Market 2008-2013 (Espicom Business Intelligence, 2009)

Due to the increase in the number of medical equipment that will be available in Saudi Arabia, it could be assumed that an outsourced management system will be required to reduce the added burden of equipment management on healthcare professionals, as well as lessen the lag time lost during equipment failure. In 2008, Saudi Arabia General Investment Authority announced that it will either privatize or outsource the management of 218 hospitals.

B) UAE

Based on GDP per capita, according to the World Health Statistics Report, UAE is among the countries with highest GDP per capita in the world; per capita spending has been evaluated to be worth US$41,390 in 2009. According to WHO Statistics 2010 Report, UAE per capita total expenditure on healthcare is the second highest in GCC after Qatar, a significant increase over the size of the expenditures between years 2000-2007. In 2006 expenditures on health were US$ 6.5 billion (WHOSIS, 2010). In 2007, the UAE invested 2.5% of its GDP for the development of its healthcare sector. In 2009, overall healthcare expenditures in

UAE totalled US$5.8 billion; 2.6% of the UAE's GDP (Espicom Business Intelligence, 2010).

In terms of the absolute value of expenditure, the Government expenditure on health per capita at exchange rate has increased. Per capita expenditures on healthcare at exchange rate have also increased from 1995-2008. It is forecasted that expenditures will increase to US$12.3 billion in 2012. The total size of the medical equipment market in 2009 amounted to US$641.5 in 2009 (Klugman, 2010).

C) Kuwait

Similar to other GCC countries, Kuwait's healthcare expenditures have been increasing. Healthcare is one of the industry sectors that have been marked for growth in the government's infrastructure development program. According to Business Monitor International, expenditure in the healthcare market is expected to grow from US$3.14 billion in 2009 to 3.5 billion in 2010 (Business Monitor International, 2010). By international standards, Kuwait has relatively weak healthcare capacity indicators; Kuwait has 19 hospital beds per 10,000 populations compared to 39 in the UK and 140 in Japan (The Middle East, 2011). This problem however is being addressed though the infrastructure development plan, 8 new public hospitals will be built generating 4800 additional beds by 2016. Expansion plans for nine hospitals are underway and will also generate 2,000 additional beds. Kuwait is one of the slower growing healthcare markets in GCC, the healthcare sector is expected to grow by 8.47% CAGR from 2009 to 2014. By 2014, it is expected that spending will reach US$1.37 billion, with the public sector contributing to 74.7% of the market growth (Business Monitor International, 2010). In 2009 Kuwait spent 3.3% of its GDP on Health. In 2009, the government contributed to 83.9% of total health expenditures in the country (Global Health Observatory, 2011).

D) Qatar

Due to its rapid economic growth and steady oil and gas prices, Qatar presents one of the most promising healthcare markets. According to Business Monitor International, Qatar's healthcare market is expected to grow from US$4.89bn in 2010 to US$5.63bn in 2011. Qatar however, is expected to grow at a rate of 11.16% CAGR reaching US$400 million in 2014 (Allianz Worldwide Care, 2011). The medical device market is expected to grow from US$169mn in 2010 to US$193mn in 2011. Healthcare expenditure is likely to be supported through further building projects as the government continues in its quest to diversify the economy and move away from its reliance on oil. An example of this is the Hamad Medical City (HMC), which, once completed in 2012, will be a self-sufficient complex, with four hospitals, as well as its own restaurant and mosque (Business Monitor International, 2010).

E) Oman

Health expenditures in Oman have increased by 16.8% between 2004 and 2009. In 2009 Oman spent 2.3% (US$1.2 billion) of its GDP on health; this amounts to US$414.6 per capita. Government expenditures as a percentage of total health expenditures were substantial; the government contributed to 84% of the total health expenditures in 2009. In addition, according to the latest figures (released in 2009), 54 hospitals of the 58 hospitals in the country, are run and owned by the government. In relation to the medical equipment market, in 2009 the market reached US$56 million (US$18.8 per capita) (Business Monitor International, 2010).

F) Bahrain

Healthcare expenditure in Bahrain has increased recently due to chronic diseases such as obesity. Bahrain ranks sixth in the world in terms of overall obesity; 28.9% of the population is classified as obese. Obesity leads to other diseases such as cardiovascular disease, which will further increase Bahrain's spending on healthcare. Bahrain's drug expenditures were valued at US$120 million in 2010, up from US$112 million in 2009 (News Medical: Research and Market, 2010).

Furthermore, overall spending on healthcare has increased from BD 64 million (~US$169.7 million) in 2001 to BD 203 million (~US$538.4 million) in 2009 (Bahrain Economic Quarterly, 2011).

4.3.2 Public Private Partnerships (PPPs) in the GCC States

Due to the rising cost of providing healthcare, leaders are trying to pass on some of the responsibility to the private sector. As such, governments are now looking for new partnerships to form with entities in the private sector. Most GCC countries have donated huge capital investments to infrastructure projects. Using their substantial capital, due to high profits from oil prices and investment income, the GCC countries can afford to invest in massive infrastructure projects without resorting to borrowing large sums of money (Frost & Sullivan, The GCC Healthcare Industry Outlook, 2009).

Businesses in the Gulf Region are focusing on projects that guarantee a stream of steady cash rather than projects that have high commercial or revenue risk. (WHO, 2008) Public private partnerships provide a very suitable solution through which private entities can leverage public investments in infrastructure using private funds. This allows public companies to gain access to knowledge, skills and technology transferred from Western companies. It also allows private companies to transfer the risks of the project development to the government entity. Private sector infrastructure in GCC will thus become more impervious to credit crunch than other markets (Frost & Sullivan, 2009).

4.3.3 New Healthcare Projects in the GCC

In the phase of the identification and pre-selection of potential projects, the government typically looks for possible ways to execute the planed task. This could be traditional ways, PPP or other way to involve the private sector (Haarlander, Buhner, Schwandt, & Schoffski, 2007).

Healthcare projects can be used to identify the countries that have the highest healthcare growth and development potential. Future standards of healthcare can be derived by analyzing the standards that the facilities intend on accomplishing.

Below is an overview of the top ten most expensive projects in the GCC based on the amount of money invested in building the medical facility (Egbert, 2009).

A) Saudi Arabia

Al Khobar Hospital

A US$55 million, 200-bed hospital, located in Al Khobar city was planed to be completed in May 2010 and should be fully financed by the Ministry of Health (Mourshed, Hediger, & Lambert, 2007).

Saud Bin Jalwaei Hospital

This hospital with an estimated cost of US$55 million hospital is located in Al Ahsa, KSA. It is also financed by the Saudi Arabian Ministry of Health. 200-bed hospital is the expected size after the completion (Mourshed, Hediger, & Lambert, 2007).

Al Mokowah Hospital

Al Mokowah Hospital is a US$24 million 100-bed hospital completed in 2009. It is located in Al Mokowah city in Saudi Arabia (Egbert, 2009).

B) United Arab Emirates

Cleveland Clinic Hospital

The hospital is a US$1.9 billion project that is set to be open in the emirate of Abu Dhabi. Cleveland Clinic Hospital was planned as the most advanced medical facility in United Arab Emirates. With 324 specialized clinics and 360 beds, it will also be amongst the largest (Egbert, 2009).

Al Mafraq Hospital

Al Mafraq hospital is located in Abu Dhabi. Although not as impressive as the Cleveland Clinic Hospital, Al Mafraq Hospital is valued at US$871 million. It is one of the oldest hospitals in Abu Dhabi. New buildings and many other modifications, including environmentally-friendly and energy-efficient designs will be added to the hospital. The entire project is expected to be completed by

2013 (Mourshed, Hediger, & Lambert, Gulf Cooperation Council Health Care: Challenges and Opportunities, 2007).

Danat Al Emarat Women & Children's Hospital

This US$150 million hospital is dedicated solely to women and children and will in fact be Abu Dhabi's first ever medical spa. (Mourshed, Hediger, & Lambert, 2007).

C) Kuwait

Jaber Ahmed Al Jaber Al Sabah Hospital

This project is valued at approximately US$1billion and is expected to open by the first quarter of 2014 in Surra, Kuwait. Along with state-of-the-art facilities and equipment, this hospital will have a private wing for VIP suites (Mourshed, Hediger, & Lambert, 2007).

Bayan Palace Health Centre

This US$54 million medical centre has already been completed and is now located in Bayan Palace in Kuwait (Egbert, 2009).

D) Qatar

Sidra Medical and Research Centre

This US$2.3 billion centre located in Qatar is scheduled to open in 2012. It was designed according to the highest international standards. The centre will provide world-class clinical care, medical education, and perform biomedical research (Alpen Capital Limited, 2009).

United Arab Emirates, and more specifically Abu Dhabi, is investing the most on healthcare projects. Saudi Arabia has distributed its investments into smaller less advanced hospitals; Qatar in comparison has invested a large sum in one state-of-the-art hospital. United Arab Emirates has made large investments in several state-of-the-art hospitals; and thus has opted to increase both the quantity and the quality of healthcare in the country. Two among the top ten most expensive projects belong to Kuwait, and as such it should be considered a very profitable healthcare market in proportion to its size. GCC countries that are not evident in the list are Bahrain and Oman, whose healthcare sectors are much less sophisticated compared to other GCC countries (Alpen Capital Limited, 2009).

4.3.4 Availability of Free Healthcare in GCC

When a government takes the responsibility of providing healthcare within a certain country or region, it is expected that there will be an increased use of healthcare facilities in these areas. Therefore, if more free healthcare facilities are available in the GCC states, then an increase in the use of healthcare and associated medical equipment could occur. Full free healthcare is predominantly provided only to GCC nationals; free healthcare is not generally available to expatriates. In addition, nationals are given health insurance from international employers to be used in private hospitals (Huges, 2003). An overview of the existing free clinics in GCC country will be given. These clinics will then be compared to clinics in countries of the West.

All of the GCC countries provide free clinics

Saudi Arabia

KSA made great efforts to provide the best healthcare for its nationals and expatriates alike. Saudi Arabia has highly subsidized public health services in the country offered either for free or for a very low cost health to residents. Free healthcare in Saudi Arabia is offered to expatriates as well (Huges, 2003).[11]

United Arab Emirates

Healthcare in the United Arab Emirates differs somewhat from that of Saudi Arabia. Although it is of the same high standards as its neighbouring country, the availability of free healthcare is not as widespread as it is in Saudi Arabia. In addition, the type of free healthcare provided varies from one emirate to the other. For instance, Abu Dhabi offers free healthcare to all nationals and limited to all expatriates, even going as far as making health insurance for employees mandatory to all employers. Dubai, on the other hand, does not have such policy

[11] Range of healthcare services is limited and might vary from year to year.

and its free clinics are only free to UAE nationals (Zawya, 2009).

Kuwait

Healthcare in Kuwait is offered to all nationals and expatriates alike. However, there is a discrepancy between the services offered to nationals and to expatriates. For nationals, free healthcare is so extensive that the country provides veterinary services for free. Free healthcare for expatriates is comparatively deficient (Helem, 2011)

Qatar

Like Saudi Arabia, Qatar previously provided all nationals and expatriates with free healthcare throughout the entire country. Unfortunately, due to rising budget concerns, the government requires all nationals and expatriates to purchase health cards. Although the prices are still very low and are at a fraction of the real costs, the change in policy was unwelcome as it was seen to have ruined the all-free system (World Health Organization, WHO, 2011).

Oman

Oman provides free healthcare as well. However, it also follows the trend of other GCC countries, where expatriates are not as fully covered as the nationals. Omani nationals receive full coverage on healthcare, without paying any fees. However, the expatriates are required to pay an annual registration fee of 1Omani Riyal (OMR) (US$2.60), and a nominal user charge of OMR 0.2 (US$0.50) per visit (EMRO, 2011).

Bahrain

Bahrain does provide free healthcare to all nationals and expatriates in the country. However, this might be a trend that resembles the problems of Qatar. The costs of healthcare in Bahrain are estimated to be more than triple by 2025, rising from the current BD 170 million (US$452 million) to BD 553 million (US$1.47 billion). This increase in costs will make it impossible to offer free healthcare, and Bahrain is forced to look into other options, such as compulsory insurance for all (Baxter, 2009).

The free healthcare systems in the GCC are under severe pressure due to rising healthcare costs. Countries such as Bahrain and Qatar were forced to abandon the "free healthcare for all" approach and find other means of maintaining healthcare. This trend is not limited to the GCC only, for the same situation occurred in European countries as well. Healthcare costs have drastically grown and countries such as Britain, France, and Switzerland are suffering just as the GCC countries are (Alpen Capital Limited, 2009).

4.3.5 The Role of Insurance

Based on multiple interviews with senior government officials and health consultants, insurance market is on the rise in the GCC countries, with many countries impliementing mandatory health insurance to expatriates. This is expected to both grow and develop the healthcare market. According to Joseph Newhouse in the first volume of his book *Health of Economics*, higher availability of health insurance or wider coverage of health insurance results in a change in behaviour towards healthcare services. This is referred to as the Moral Hazard in which, "People with health insurance tend to see the doctors more often, and to use costly treatments even if the benefits are small" (Newhouse, 2000). The Moral Hazard also affects doctors, according to Newhouse, "Since costs are not borne by patients, it is easier for doctors to suggest more expensive treatments"; these two changes in the behaviour of doctors and patients result in an overall increase in health expenditures. The Moral Hazard also contributes to the growth and development of the healthcare market by increasing the supply of new technology which would not be affordable without insurance (Imoh & Mutshinda, 2010). According to Alpen Capital, GCC health expenditure per capita is expected to grow faster than the global average due to increased health insurance, and income levels (Alpen Capital Limited, 2009).

European countries and the United States of America only offer conventional insurance, GCC countries in comparison offer both conventional ("western") insurance, and an Islamic version of insurance called Takaful. Insurance plays a very important role in the healthcare industry and is widely used within GCC. Expatriates use either conventional insurance or Takaful. The GCC countries are increasingly beginning to use the conventional insurance options.

A) Conventional Insurance

The insurance industry in the GCC plays an extremely important role in affecting the quality of healthcare that an insurance holder can access. Not all the GCC countries offer free healthcare to all its citizens. Due to lack of free healthcare, the role of insurance is significant in the healthcare industry in the GCC states.

The insurance industry in the GCC has been growing at a very high rate. In fact, insurance premiums in the GCC have reached US$10.6 billion in 2009, a recorded 28 % increase from the previous. Compared to the worldwide average of 3.4 %, the growth rate of insurance in the GCC is very high. The penetration rate however is very low, amounting to 0.6 % and 2 % in Saudi Arabia and the United Arab Emirates respectively. Penetration rates range from 5 to 15 % in the United States and Europe; this indicates that there is still a great potential for growth in the insurance industries of the GCC states (Al Mashni, 2010).

A trend has been observed in which GCC residents only purchase insurance when it is made mandatory. Hence, Dubai's Health Chief plans on creating a policy that makes health insurance a requirement for all of Dubai's residents; Abu Dhabi has already implemented a similar policy. Employers in Abu Dhabi are required to send a fixed medical coverage monetary payment on behalf of every employee to the government. If this policy is implemented throughout UAE, and in other GCC states, overall demand for healthcare will increase as more advanced and expensive healthcare options become more affordable, and thus accessible to residents (McGinley, 2010).

The insurance industry, specifically health insurance, is considered to be on the brink of rapid growth. The concept of health insurance is still somewhat new to the region, as such penetration rates are far below the potential available in GCC states, and are expected to grow in the following years. A growth in health insurance will thus lead to the growth of the healthcare industry (McGinley, 2010).

B) Islamic Insurance (Takaful)

The word "Takaful" is an Arabic term for "guaranteeing each other." Takaful is similar to conventional insurance, where one makes payments in order to be financially covered in the event of an unfortunate accident. The conventional insurance concept however, is forbidden by most Islamic scholars due to the fact that it involves interest, gambling, and uncertainty; all of which are not permissible in 'Shariah' (Islamic Law). Takaful involves a mutual agreement among a group of people that choose to donate a certain sum of money in order to protect one another in the event of an accident to any parties within the agreement. In conventional insurance concept, the insurance providers can profit from an insurance holder's premiums if no accident occurs. Critical to the acceptability of Takaful in Islam, is that the money donated by the parties is only used in the event of an accident or other medical necessity (Ayub, 2003).

The Takaful industry in the GCC states has been predicted to reach US$3.519 billion (Dh12.91) by the end of 2010. Takaful's compound annual growth rate (CAGR) is expected to be 16.1 per cent during from year 2009 to year 2012 (Pathak, 2010). It has been predicted that the industry will grow to be worth about US$4 billion in the near future (Zawya, 2007). The Takaful industry, along with Islamic banking, is growing at very high rates in order to cater to Shariah (Islamic Law) compliant banking and insurance practices. It has been estimated that 70.4 % of all Takaful business in the world, is based in the GCC (Pathak, 2010). Therefore, it is safe to assume that about 70 % of the growth in Takaful occurs in the GCC states.

Both Takaful and conventional health insurance are growing at very high rates in GCC states. As an industry complementary to the health insurance industry, this growth could indicate that high growth will also be stimulated in the healthcare industry of GCC states.

4.3.6 Challenges in GCC Countries Healthcare Sectors

Healthcare sectors in GCC countries face a number of challenges which have created a gap between healthcare supply and demand. Each of these challenges, as well as the resulting projected increase in demand, is described.

A) Lack of Sustainability of the Welfare Model

Within the healthcare sector, the GCC governments employ the Welfare Model. Most of the healthcare within each of the Gulf States is either highly or completely subsidized. Full free healthcare coverage is provided to nationals, and partial or full free healthcare coverage is provided to expatriates. Governments in the GCC provide healthcare for expatriates at a fraction of the cost that they bear (Mourshed, Hediger, & Lambert, 2007). Several factors have lead to high demand for an increase in healthcare expenditures thereby threatening the sustainability of the welfare model.

- The governments of the GCC governments face added healthcare expenses due to the high growth in the number of expatriates. A 3.0% CAGR is expected until 2015, this growth rate will then decrease to 1.8% CAGR. As a result, it is projected that by 2025, the size of GCC's population will be doubled from its size in 2009. There has also been a reduction in infant mortality rates, further contributing to population growth (Mourshed, Hediger, & Lambert, 2007).
- There has also been an increase in chronic illnesses, especially those related cardiovascular disease. Compared to the rest of the world, there is an exceedingly high rate of people who suffer from Type 2 diabetes and obesity. Lifestyle diseases such as high blood pressure, heart disease, and diabetes contribute to approximately 50% of all deaths in the Gulf Region in 2006 (Frost & Sullivan, 2009). 40% of GCC nationals are obese. A study conducted by UAE Ministry of Health and the World Health Organization in 2001 revealed that "25 percent of UAE citizens suffer from diabetes (as compared with an average of 5 to 7 percent globally). This figure rises to an unprecedented level of 40 percent for those aged 60 or above" (Mourshed, Hediger, & Lambert, 2007, p. 56). Obesity and chronic illnesses are alarming in Saudi Arabia, according to the results of a survey by Saudi Diabetes and Endocrine Association (SDEA) in 2010, 70% of the Saudi population is alarmingly obese. In 2009, 6.2% of the patient visits to the Ministry of Health medical facilities were related to

diabetes (NCB, 2011). Health complications related to diabetes and obesity will contribute to an increase in medical expenses in the future. In 2007, it has been forecasted that health-care delivery in the GCC countries will cost about US$60 billion by 2025; five times the cost of healthcare delivery in 2009. Cardiovascular disease will specifically become an enormous cost burden on the GCC; it is predicted to increase from 12% percent of total healthcare expenditure to 24% (double the amount) (Mourshed, Hediger, & Lambert, 2007). Heart diseases related to diabetes were responsible for 31% of all deaths in 2008. Currently, public healthcare system focuses on general treatment; there is a gap in the availability of specialized public healthcare facilities that are needed to compensate for the increase in chronic diseases (Frost & Sullivan, 2009).

- Due to advances in healthcare provision in the GCC nations, life expectancy has increased which has lead to a higher number of elderly people. For example, the population above the age of 65 is expected to increase to more than seven times its size in 2009 (Mourshed, Hediger, & Lambert, 2007). Accordingly healthcare must be provided to a larger number of older people who generally have higher demand for healthcare. According to Mukesh Chawla, in his book, *Health Care spending in the New EU Member States: Controlling Costs and Improving Quality,* "Elderly people (above 65) have higher average demand for medical care in their later years in terms of ambulatory, inpatient, and chronic care"; therefore an increase in the aging segment of the population will lead to an increase in healthcare expenditures and further straining the welfare model (Chawla, 2007).

- Due to the previous factors, it has been predicted that there will be an increase in demand for treatment and hospital beds. Demand for treatment will increase by 240%. Cardiovascular disease specifically within the GCC countries will increase by 419%. Demand for treatment related to diabetes will increase by 323%. The next graph forecasts the percentage increase in demand for treatment (by type of disease) in the GCC countries from 2009 to 2025. (Mourshed, Hediger, & Lambert, 2007)

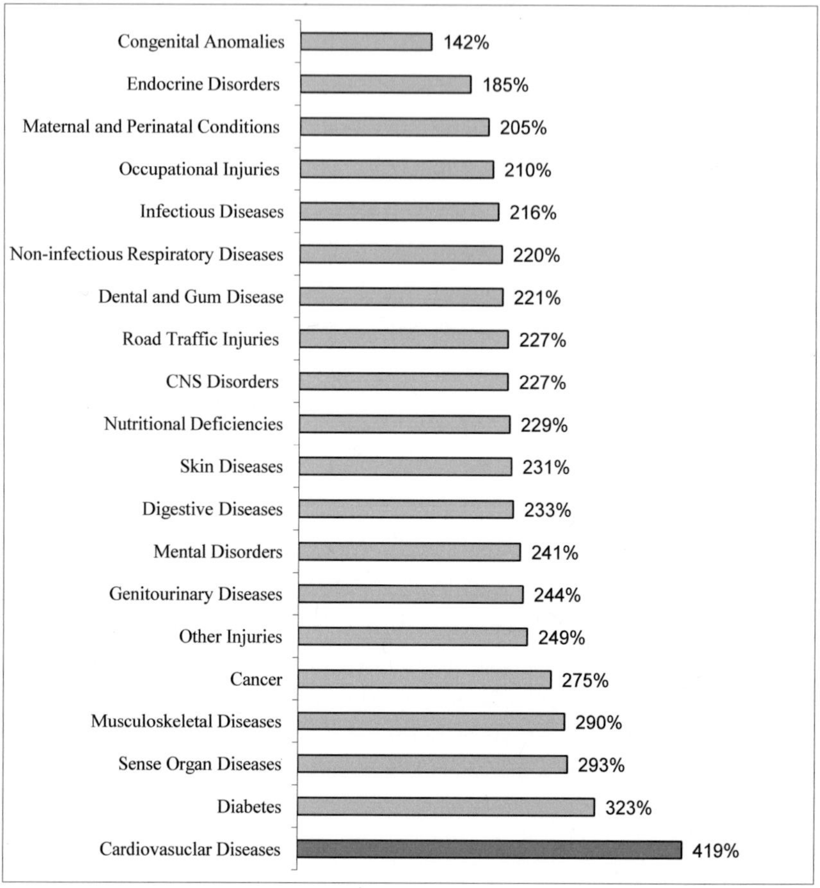

Figure 15: Projected Percent Increase in Treatment Demand in GCC Countries by 2025 (Mourshed, Hediger, & Lambert, 2007)

Traditionally, the GCC countries have had the luxury of ignoring such lack of sustainability in government programs due to vast oil and gas revenues; however, due to the reasons described above, the welfare model has grown to become far too expensive and unsustainable in the GCC countries (Shediac, Hashemi, & Bhatia, 2009).

B) Underdeveloped Private Healthcare Market

The GCC healthcare sectors are overly dependent on government funding; government hospitals have a capacity rate of approximately 80% (Alpen Capital Limited, 2009). Within the GCC, the governments have always provided the residents with public hospitals that provide cheap treatment for patients. Low demand for private healthcare has resulted in the underdevelopment of the private healthcare market within GCC states. In one of the GCC countries, private hospitals have been reported to operate at 10% to 40% of their capacity (Mourshed, Hediger, & Lambert, 2007). According to Forst & Sullivan, "Growth of the private healthcare sector in the region especially in Saudi Arabia and Oman, has stagnated in large part because of free public services" (Frost & Sullivan, 2009, p. 16); this could be in part due to a trend where patients pay private providers for diagnosis and then obtain treatment in public medical facilities (Mourshed, Hediger, & Lambert, 2007).

According to interviews conducted with healthcare consultancies and senior figures in UAE Government, while the private healthcare market is underdeveloped in size, it is more advanced in terms of healthcare delivery (UAE Government, 2011). While the public healthcare system focuses on general treatments, private hospitals tend to offer either comprehensive services or specialized care. This could indicate that the development of the private healthcare delivery market could lead to a substantial increase in the quality of healthcare in the region as well as an increase in the supply of specialized treatments.

The GCC governments are trying to encourage the growth of the private healthcare sector using numerous methods. In Saudi Arabia for example, the process of obtaining financing through lending institutions has been eased for the private healthcare sector players. Health insurance has also been introduced as a means of increasing expenditure in the private healthcare sector (NCB, 2011). Dubai Healthcare City, a healthcare city that houses healthcare providers and other entities within the healthcare industry, was developed to attract private players by offering benefits such as 100% ownership rights (a national partner is not required), no restrictions on capital, trade barriers or quotas, and uncomplicated company registration and legal framework (DHCC Press Coverage, 2011). Public Private Partnerships (PPPs) schemes (covered later in this paper) have also been introduced as a method of the increasing private participation; although according to the interview with a senior healthcare advisor, legal regulation have to be adjusted in order to promote PPPs.

Healthcare legal complexities and a general lack of healthcare regulation is a key challenge facing private healthcare providers. According to Frost & Sullivan, "Majority of the GCC countries require more aggressive reforms and government regulations in areas like health insurance, clinical trials, medical devices and pharmaceuticals" (Frost & Sullivan, The GCC Healthcare Industry Outlook, 2009, p. 8). Based on interviews conducted with multiple health consultants, health financing institutions and senior government officials in UAE, there is a general lack of healthcare regulation in regards to operations, healthcare standards, and the establishment of private healthcare facilities (HC Consultancy 1, 2011). This translates into a lack of transparency, in Saudi Arabia for example corporate players regard the healthcare sector being rather complex and as such are reluctant to penetrate the market (NCB, 2011) (Mourshed, Hediger, & Lambert, 2007).

C) Lack of Equipment Knowledge among Healthcare Professionals

GCC countries have been investing heavily into their healthcare systems. These investments include the purchase of state-of-the-art medical equipment, and construction of new hospitals. While the medical staffs are provided with the most recent technology, due to a lack of knowledge and training, healthcare professionals may not use the equipment properly (Government Health, 2011). This in turn contributes to patient misdiagnosis and to an overall reduction in the quality of healthcare provision. There is a prevalent trend in the GCC countries in which residents opt for treatment in other non-GCC countries (Mourshed, Hediger, & Lambert, 2007). According to a report published by McKinsey, UAE residents spent AED 7.2 billion (US$1.9 billion) on treatment abroad, mainly due to lack of confidence in the local healthcare system and due to the high cost of treatment (Saberi, 2010).

D) Expatriates Greatly Outnumber Nationals

The GCC countries suffer from a healthcare workforce crisis. In UAE for example, the expatriate workforce constitutes over 80%[12] of the healthcare workforce (Mourshed, Hediger, & Lambert, 2007). In GCC, 75% of physicians are expatriates and 80% of nurses are expatriates (Frost & Sullivan, 2009). According to an interview conducted with a senior advisor to the Government of Dubai as part of this study, there are high turnover rates in UAE's healthcare workforce, as many expatriate healthcare professionals view the GCC as a stepping stone to other healthcare markets and as a temporary home. High-turnover in physicians, for example, has led to discontinuity in the relationship between physician and patient which poses a major problem. In addition, many of the young healthcare professionals who train in the UAE leave, which results to knowledge loss. One of the main challenges that the GCC countries face is access to healthcare/ medical knowledge and experience. Attracting high quality, knowledgeable healthcare professionals is a problem. According to the interview conducted with a senior healthcare advisor in UAE, attracting knowledgeable expatriate professionals is challenging as most knowledgeable professionals are successful in their own countries and as such have no intentions to work abroad (Government Health, 2011). Saudi Arabia also faces the same problem, turnover rates for nurses in Saudi is approximately 2 years (NCB, 2011).

The repercussions of a heavy dependence on the expatriate workforce emphasize the need for developing the national workforce by promoting the growth of the medical education system. GCC governments have intensified their effort to increase the number of medical teaching and research institutions in the region through local medical university projects. Now it is estimated that the GCC has about fourteen senior medical institutions and faculties. These are King Saud University of Health Sciences in KSA, the Faculty of Medicine and Health Sciences (FMHS) in UAE University in UAE, the Faculty of Medicine in Sultan Qaboos University (SQU) in the Sultanate of Oman, the College of Medicine and

[12] Based on: 'Source of human resources in the healthcare sector, 2001-02'. Provided by the Ministry of Health for expatriate physicians and nurses.

Medical Sciences (CMMS) in the Arabian Gulf University in Bahrain, the Weill Cornell Medical College in Qatar, and the Faculty of Medicine in Kuwait University in Kuwait (Hamdy, et al., 2010). Moreover, GCC governments have been heavily investing in medical scholarship schemes for nationals (Alpen Capital Limited, 2009).

E) Higher Expectations for Healthcare

According to McKinsey Satisfaction survey, GCC patients have higher expectations for the healthcare than what is being provided. This general discontent is a result of direct patient experience. Public hospitals bear the brunt of patient criticism and dissatisfaction due to limited appointment hours, long waiting periods, as well as uncomfortable and unattractive facilities (Mourshed, Hediger, & Lambert, 2007). According to a survey conducted in Kuwait, based on results from 1,255 patients improvements need to be made in regards to "...physicians rendering more attention to the patient's beliefs, anxieties, and opinion regarding the management plan, skill training to physicians for better communication and practice nurse services" (Bu-Alayyan, Mostafa, Al-Etaibi, Sorkhou, Al-Taher, & Al-Weqayyan, 2008, pp. 25-30). Thus, it is highly important that uniform quality standards are identified and implemented in GCC healthcare facilities at the country level.

5. MES as a Business Opportunity in GCC

The purpose of this chapter is to analyze how the challenges described and identified in the previous chapter can be converted into business opportunities for an MES program. In order to asses areas for MES growth, first the GCC healthcare market will be evaluated for possible areas of opportunities, and then the industry will be analyzed using Porter's Five Forces.

5.1 MES Healthcare Market Opportunities in GCC

Healthcare spending is expected to increase to US$60 billion by the year 2025, from the US$12 billion estimated today (Mourshed, Hediger, & Lambert, 2007). Nevertheless, the GCC countries are not prepared to accommodate for this increase in healthcare demand. The main reasons for this is the GCC members populations' reliance on public hospitals, and the underdevelopment of the private healthcare sector in the GCC, as well as a number of other facts described in the *Challenges in the GCC Countries' Healthcare Sectors* section of this report.

Opportunities can be created in five main areas:

- Healthcare delivery
- Support services
- Health insurance
- Reimbursement systems
- Contracting with private providers (Mourshed, Hediger, & Lambert, 2007)

5.1.1 Healthcare Delivery

The development of a primary care management system for cardiovascular disease and chronic illnesses such as diabetes and obesity represents a significant growth opportunity. According to McKinsey GCC Report, the direct healthcare costs in the GCC region are expected to quintuple by 2025 to US$60 billion from US$12 billion, with health risk factors, ageing, population growth and medical inflation contributing to the cost escalation. In particular, costs in the field of cardiology will increase to US$15 billion, forming approximately 24% of the total costs of the healthcare sector (Mourshed, Hediger, & Lambert, 2007). The graph below provides a forecast of the development of the healthcare sector expenditures of the GCC countries by the type of disease.

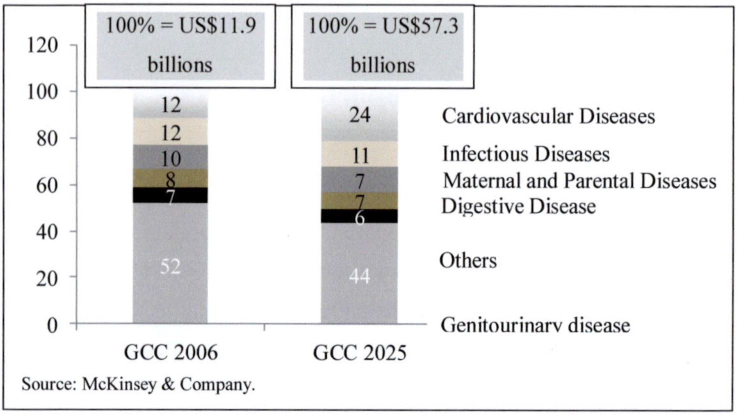

Figure 16: Growth in Types of Disease in GCC 2006-2025 (Mourshed, Hediger, & Lambert, 2007)

GCC countries are already recruiting companies from the private sector to manage primary care medical facilities. Healthcare growth opportunities are also available areas where healthcare infrastructure is underdeveloped. The GCC disease demand profile indicates that there will be considerable demand for oncology treatments, however very few medical facilities in the GCC countries are equipped to provide these. (Mourshed, Hediger, & Lambert, 2007) Oncology treatment represents the 5th highest demand increase by 2025. Facilities that provide cancer treatment, as well as acute rehabilitation, elderly care, home care, occupational therapy, and speech therapy are underdeveloped in GCC countries and as such also represent growth opportunities (NCB, 2011). Outpatient surgery centres could also be developed to reduce the average length of hospital stay, and thereby reduce patient dissatisfaction, and increase patient turnover (Mourshed, Hediger, & Lambert, 2007).

5.1.2 Supplementary Services

Recent growth in the healthcare sector has caused the GCC governments to focus on policies and medical facility regulation systems that ensure and promote high standard healthcare delivery. GCC countries have little experience in this area, as such; they likely recruit private international entities and government institutions in developed countries as for support. Private entities are likely to help governments define the organizational functions of the regulatory body (policy maker), as well as set the required standards for healthcare providers (faculties), healthcare professionals, and payers. This opens the path for private IT providers to offer management services that promote transparency; clinical quality reporting, financial management at the procedure, departmental, and institutional level. The creation of transparent reporting systems aid decision makers at medical institutions in the evaluation of current performance, and in the identification of areas for improvement (Frost & Sullivan, 2009). The GCC governments have attempted to set these policies in the past through the use of private institutions but were faced with several challenges that they are now resolving:

- Due to a lack of systematic channels, a referral system, and out-crowding by the public sector, patient threshold volume in private hospitals cannot be guaranteed. Patient threshold volume is critical to maintain steady profits for investments in necessary high cost medical equipment (i.e. medical equipment required for heart surgery, and in radiology departments). In addition, high patient volume increases medical staff experience, and knowledge resulting in more successful medical and surgical results (NCB, 2011). This challenge however is likely to be resolved within the next few years as the GCC governments have begun promoting the private healthcare sector by paying for the patient (GCC nationals) expenses incurred in private medical facilities rather than providing the medical services in public medical institutions (Mourshed, Hediger, & Lambert, 2007).

- Retaining a sufficient number of trained clinical staff to support growing populations is problematic. Expatriates form the overwhelming majority of medical staff. They view the GCC countries as a temporary home, and as such, there is a very high clinical staff employment turnover. This makes it very hard to retain experienced and knowledgeable medical staffs that are capable of delivering high-quality healthcare services. The GCC governments as a result have started promoting the employment of nationals in the healthcare sector by encouraging international medical colleges and universities to open branches in their countries (i.e. Cornell's undergraduate medical education program in Qatar and the Royal College of Surgeons of Ireland's postgraduate facilities in Bahrain) (Chawla, 2007).
- Transitioning away from the welfare model and reducing government subsidization of healthcare will cause health insurance providers to bear more health costs, resulting in a reduction in profits earned by these entities. The GCC governments lack the knowledge required to run complex healthcare systems. This gives room for international health insurance providers to enter healthcare market in the GCC and provide services such as processing and providing claims, teaching providers to issue claims, and to reimburse them (Chawla, 2007).

5.1.3 Contracting With a Private Provider

There is a shortage of hospital and primary care management skills. This gives private institutions the opportunity to profit from managing hospitals and primary care facilities, as well as laboratories and pharmacies. Private institutions will thus profit by earning cash incentives when they meet performance targets and care quality standards. There have been situations in which a government will auction one of its hospitals to the private firm that places the lowest bid. This means that the country will put the hospital up for auction and place the bid at the hospital's current budget. The private firm that places the lowest bid, while still adhering to a specified quality and standard, will be able to manage that hospital (Chawla, 2007). According to McKinsey & Company, a GCC government has started accepting bids (most GCC member state governments select private players through a bidding process) for managing its secondary care healthcare facilities, however the constraints outlined by the government have made it unattractive for other private players to go through a similar process (Mourshed, Hediger, & Lambert, Gulf Cooperation Council Health Care: Challenges and Opportunities, 2007). For example on the 14th of May 2011, the UAE government announced the launch of its second phase of hospital accreditation in which it commissioned Mehalek, a US international assessment group, to assess the current status of the health services and medical practices in the facilities belonging to its Ministry of Health by applying international standards to evaluate all hospitals and health centres (WAM, 2011).

In Saudi Arabia, most hospitals are built on a turnkey basis by foreign contractors who recruit medical professionals and provide the medical equipment for the hospital. When the contractor changes, however, new equipment must be purchased to suit the standards and capabilities of the new medical professionals that are hired as a result of the change (Mufti, 2002). The old equipment thus becomes obsolete. This reflects a need for a system through which the technology purchased has the capacity to withstand technology upgrades. An MES contract could provide such a system; rather than purchase new equipment, the MES provider is capable of upgrading the equipment that it produces. Depending on the terms of the MES contract, the MES provider could also provide the new equipment at a discounted price. The hospital could also sell back the equipment to the MES provider. Furthermore, if agreed upon in the contract, MES providers can train medical staff on how to effectively use new technology (Asteral, 2011).

There is a lack of coordination between agencies in the health sector in Saudi Arabia. This has led to the unnecessary purchase of expensive medical equipment. Duplication of resources is one of the main factors that have led to the escalation of health expenses. Depending on the contract, an MES provider can determine the equipment that best suits the hospitals needs, and procure it for the hospital. Depending on the type of MES model that is used, the hospital may not even own the equipment and as such the hospital would not have to bear the risk in terms of the cost of technology obsolescence and depreciation costs (Mourshed, Hediger, & Lambert, 2007).

5.1.4 Reimbursement System

Within the next five to ten years, it is expected that the GCC countries will introduce a basic benefits package that will be available, for free, to all the GCC nationals. The GCC governments strictly control the premiums that can be charged to ensure their affordability for low income expatriates who comprise the majority of expatriates in the GCC countries. As such, if private entities attempt to provide a similar basic benefits package to expatriates, they would have to survive on a very tight profit margin (Mourshed, Hediger, & Lambert, 2007). Unless the entity has exclusive right to a particular region, private providers would not have the incentive required to enter the healthcare markets in the GCC countries. An opportunity can be created in this area through the development of a premium benefits package. This package targets high-income expatriates by providing a "high-end" benefits package and include elective plastic surgery and dental coverage. The market penetration rates forecasted indicate that 4%-5% of the population would invest in this type of benefits package. Due to the profitability of these packages, more private healthcare providers might be attracted to the GCC healthcare market (Alpen Capital Limited, 2009).

5.2 Porter's Five Forces Analysis: Attractiveness of MES in the GCC

Drawing from the analysis of the GCC's Healthcare market and the information obtained about MES programs, an analysis[13] of the attractiveness of the GCC medical equipment and services market will be performed using Porter's Five Forces (Porter, 2008). The model was developed by Michael Porter who is considered as an authority on competitive strategy (Wheelen & Hunger, 2009). Under this model, five forces that affect the industry are evaluated:

- Threat of substitutes

[13] Based on the most important/ chosen point of views.

- Bargaining power of the buyers
- Bargaining power of the suppliers
- Threat of new entrants
- Intensity of the competition

The strength of the forces determines the profit that can be realized in the industry analyzed. The stronger each force is the harder it is for the company to raise its prices and increase its profit margin (Wheelen & Hunger, 2009). The ultimate goal of the analysis is to evaluate the profitability of an MES program for the medical equipment industries in the GCC countries. The industry analyzed is the medical equipment industry in the GCC countries. The scope of the medical equipment industry includes the associated equipment services provided by medical equipment providers. A medical equipment provider within this context is defined as the business entity that both produces and directly or indirectly distributes its products. The industry is as such being evaluated for the potential it may hold for running an MES program. The scope of the analysis is therefore limited geographically to microeconomic environmental factors and company operations that occur specifically in the GCC countries.

5.2.1 Threat of Substitutes

A substitute product is a product that is different from the one the company is providing but can satisfy the same need. According to Porter, a substitute limits the potential returns from an industry by placing a price ceiling on the prices firms can charge (Wheelen & Hunger, 2009). The assumption made in this case is that the industry's consumers are price sensitive. While there are very few substitutes to medical equipment, the services that may be provided by medical equipment providers such as maintenance, inventory management, among others, can be substitutes. These activities can be done in-house, or they could be outsourced to other businesses that are specialized in each of these services.

Furthermore, third party equipment providers also pose a threat as they can both offer the equipment and the equipment services provided by an MES provider. The number of such substitutes (third party equipment vendors, specialized businesses) could pose a major threat if customers do not realize main benefits of an MES program, cost avoidance of multiple service, and equipment contracts. Independent Service Providers (ISOs) however are completely independent. They contract rather than partner with all of the OEMs in the market and thus act as an unbiased on-point of access for multiple equipment brands and the services associated with them.

Alternative medicine/ therapy options may serve as a substitute for therapeutic procedures performed by medical equipment. According to a survey conducted by the Dubai Healthcare City (DHCC) in 2006, 28% of people in the UAE had some form of alternative therapy during the preceding 12 months while 48% had used alternative therapy at some point in their lifetime (Zain & Shaaban, 2009). Before a patient opts for alternative therapy, he/ she must first be diagnosed with a specific disease/ disorder using traditional methods. Hence, the probability that there are products available in the GCC which could equally replace diagnostic imaging equipment is very low. Considering all the factors, the threat posed by substitutes to an MES program is considered to be high.

5.2.2 Bargaining Power of Buyers

According to Porter, buyers affect the industry though their ability to pull down prices (price negotiation power), bargain for higher quality or more services, and pit competitors against each other (Wheelen & Hunger, 2009). Buyers are powerful if they purchase a large portion of the seller's products. According to Porter, if the buyer contributes to a large portion of the seller's products then the buyer has high bargaining power (Wheelen & Hunger, 2009). If there are a large number of suppliers, then the buyer's power also increases. The medical equipment industry in the GCC is relatively concentrated. There are three large multinational medical equipment providers that dominate the market in GCC countries: General Electric, Philips, and Siemens. These companies provide their equipment and services to medical facilities throughout the GCC countries. As such there are not any individual buyers (medical facilities) that contribute to a large portion of the seller's (medical equipment providers) profits. In regards to concentration of the industry and fragmented nature of buyers of medical equipment, the power of the buyers over the seller is low.

If the buyer has high potential to integrate backwards by producing the sellers' product, then the buyers bargaining power increases (Wheelen & Hunger, 2009). Considering the high capital requirements needed to manufacture medical equipment, there is research and development expenditures, and knowledge and expertise required to compete in the medical equipment industry. Regardless of their size, it is highly unlikely that medical facilities in the GCC have the potential to integrate backwards. The average amount that GE, Philips and Siemens spent on research and development for their healthcare sectors is US$3.8 billion p.a.; GE Healthcare spent US$1 billion in 2008[14], Philips Healthcare Solutions spent US$2.3 billion in 2010, and Siemens Healthcare spent US$1.6 billion in 2010 (GE, 2011) (Philips, 2010) (Siemens, 2010). Porter indicates that if the buyer's switching costs are low, then their bargaining power over the supplier is high (Wheelen & Hunger, 2009). A medical facility's switching costs (cost of changing the medical equipment and services provider) varies depending on the nature of the purchase agreement; generally switching costs tend to be high. If the medical facility has an exclusive contract and chooses to switch to another medical equipment and services supplier before the end of the term of the contract, switching costs are likely to be high due to the high financial penalties that may be imposed. If, however, the medical facility has a onetime purchase agreement with the supplier, then switching costs are relatively lower. In both cases, the hospital incurs high sunk costs.

According to Porter, if the products purchased from the seller constitute a large portion of the buyer's costs, then the buyer will turn to competitors for cheaper products. Supplies contribute to 30% of the hospital's expenses (Lane, Longstreth, & Nixon, 2001). Equipment cost contributes to 60% of a hospital's project cost, where 50% of this is dedicated to biomedical equipment (Chandriani, 2010).

A buyer's price sensitivity with respect to buyer's profit margin has a high effect on the buyer's bargaining power, if the buyer has a low profit margin then the

[14] For the years 2010- 2012 GE announced an exceptional R&D program. (GE, 2011)

buyer will be very sensitive to cost and service differences. This increases the buyer's bargaining power. Hospitals generally operate on tight profit margins. The price sensitivity of hospitals in the GCC depends on their ownership and profitability structure. In the GCC, public hospitals generally offer free healthcare for nationals and healthcare at highly subsidized rates for expatriates. These hospitals are run with high government budgets. In 2005, the GCC governments spent about US$9 billion running public health-care facilities and reimbursing their citizens for care received abroad (Mourshed, Hediger, & Lambert, 2007). Due to rising healthcare costs, GCC governments have become more adamant about controlling how hospital budgets are being used. In the UAE for example, according to BMI, medical device expenditure as a percentage of total health expenditure is expected to fall from 6.5% in 2008 to 5.3% in 2013 as authorities pursue the best prices (Business Monitor International, 2009). Therefore, it can be expected that government hospitals will become more price sensitive. Private facilities in the GCC receive only 25% of all healthcare spending (as reimbursements for nationals or due to high government stake), thus private facilities not reimbursed or subsidized by the government have fewer patients and lower revenues than those that are. Non-government affiliated private hospitals operate at 10% to 40% of capacity, and as such are run on very tight profit margins (Saberi, 2010). Charity hospitals are funded by humanitarian foundations, and as such have variable income and run on very low funds. With regards to price sensitivity, healthcare providers are considered to have high bargaining power.

According to Porter, if the purchased product is unimportant to the final quality or price of the purchased product, then the buyer has higher bargaining power than the supplier (Wheelen & Hunger, 2009). The quality of the medical equipment and medical equipment services procured is essential to providing high quality healthcare. For example, hazy images produced by low quality diagnostic imaging equipment could lead to misdiagnosing patients. Acquiring more advanced medical equipment, such as a higher resolution MRI for example, could allow the hospital to increase the fee charged for an MRI exam, thus leading to added revenues. In this regard, it could be concluded that the buyer's bargaining power is lower than that of the supplier. Taking into account all of the factors evaluated for the buyer's bargaining power, it could be concluded, that the hospital and the MES provider would have almost equal bargaining power.

5.2.3 Bargaining Power of Suppliers

The bargaining power of the MES provider's suppliers is analyzed in this section. Suppliers in an industry retain power from their ability to raise the seller's (MES provider's) input prices as well as from their ability to reduce the quality of the goods and services that are purchased from them. According to Porter, there are five factors that affect the power of the supplier. A supplier has high bargaining power over the seller when the supplier's industry is concentrated, the product being supplied is unique, substitutes are not readily available, suppliers are able to integrate forward and compete with directly with the seller, and when the seller only purchases a small quantity of the supplier's production volume (Wheelen & Hunger, 2009).

The bargaining power of medical equipment manufacturer's varies according to the importance of the inputs that these suppliers provide to the manufacturer. If medical imaging devices are taken as an example, the power of the supplier of minor production inputs (i.e. bolts) is low due to the absence of all of the factors previously mentioned. Major production inputs are either produced by the equipment manufacturer, or bought from another supplier (at times the supplier is another OEM). Major inputs for an MRI scanner for example, are manufactured separately, and then assembled. The major components of an MRI device are superconducting electromagnets, a gradient system consisting of three coils, a radiofrequency (RF) transmitter, RF receiver, a control computer, an array processor, a main/ host computer, and peripheral devices (i.e. magnet cooling system) (Weishaupt, Köchli, & Marinček, 2006). Suppliers of the components both affect the quality of the final product, and have high negotiation power. Three companies dominate the medical imaging equipment market in GCC countries: General Electric, Philips and Siemens. These companies produce most of the major components in-house. They also act as major suppliers for these inputs. GE, Philips and Siemens globally dominate the superconductive magnet market (Abetti & Haldar, 2009). Most of these companies neither produce nor assemble their products in GCC; rather they ship the devices into the GCC countries from their designated production plants, and distribute them (in most cases) through an exclusive local distributor (National Institute for Foreign Trade, 2011). Considering the scope of manufacturing operations within the GCC, the bargaining power of suppliers is not relevant.

Distributors should be considered within the scope of the bargaining power of suppliers, as they are considered vital to providing the final product of the MES provider in the GCC countries. In UAE, for example, companies that export medical equipment are required to have a local representative or distributor. UAE's market for medical equipment in distributing a specific brand is monopolistic; there is one distributor who sells a special product and a special brand (National Institute for Foreign Trade, 2011). Similar practices and policies are followed in the rest of the GCC countries. Thus, if distributors are to be considered within the scope of a supplier, the power of suppliers is moderate in the GCC.

5.2.4 Threat of New Entrants

New entrants bring in more volume (capacity) in to the market, dilute market share, use up substantial resources that are also being used by companies already present in the market; therefore, they are considered to be a threat to these companies (Wheelen & Hunger, 2009). The threat of entry depends on the presence or absence of market entry barrier. Porter specified six entry barriers: economies of scale, product differentiation, capital requirements, switching costs, access to distribution channels, cost disadvantages (independent of size), and government policies (GE Healthcare, 2010). Other than the original equipment manufacturer (OEM) , two other types of entities are capable of providing MES programs or programs that are very similar to an MES program; small service providers (these are defined as companies that provide a service for just one modality), and large independent service organizations (ISOs) (Millennium Research Group, 2011).

Considering the scope of this analysis, an evaluation of economies of scale in production is considered for entities that intend to be OEMs based in GCC countries; the services aspect of the medical equipment industry, from this standpoint, is therefore irrelevant. OEMs that provide an MES program typically tend to be those that produce medical imaging devices. According to Porter, economies of scale represent a cost advantage for companies that are present in the market and therefore act as a barrier to entry (GE Healthcare, 2010). While cost advantages have been achieved, competition among medical imaging equipment manufacturers is not based on achieving cost advantages; rather it is based on differentiation through product innovation and patenting. Product differentiation acts as an entry barrier due to high product loyalty and brand identification. Differentiation is the ability to provide unique value to customers by offering a product with better quality, features and service than competitors (Miltenburg, 2005). Thus, entry barriers are high in product differentiation.

In the medical equipment and services industry, significant investments in research and development are required in order to manufacture high quality products that could compete with the companies present in the market. High capital requirements, according to Porter represent a barrier to entry; research and development budgets run up to billions of dollars.[15] Setting up and running medical imaging equipment production facilities require substantial capital investment.

Small medical equipment service companies and ISOs do not manufacture medical equipment and therefore require significantly less initial capital. While these entities many not be capable of providing the full scope of services provided in an MES program run by the OEM, the services they do provide could act as substitutes to an MES program. Therefore, their entry into the industry should be considered a threat.

OEMs and ISOs that operate globally could choose to enter the medical equipment and services markets in the GCC countries. Government policy, according to Porter could act as a barrier to entry; governments can limit entry

[15] GE Healthcare spent $1 billion in 2008, Philips Healthcare Solutions spent $2.3 billion in 2010, and Siemens Healthcare spent $1.6 billion in 2010 (GE, 2011) (Philips, 2010) (Siemens, 2011).

into an industry through implementing policies that restrict/ restrain business activities. Most of the GCC countries have government policies that encourage foreign investment. In the UAE for example, free zones allow easy access to favourable locations for production facilities and nearby logistics companies which further increases the threat of new entry (U.S.-U.A.E. Business Council, 2011). There are government policies however that act as a barrier to foreign investment; foreign ownership limits and licensing delays are among the main barriers to foreign investment in the GCC (Arnold, 2011). In addition, a local distributor is generally required in most GCC countries.

Switching costs as explained earlier tend to be high, variations in switching costs occur depending on the terms of the service/ purchase contract. Access to distribution channels could be difficult in the GCC countries. In most GCC countries, a local distributor is required. In the UAE, medical equipment is distributed through exclusive local distributors; each distributor distributes one brand exclusively to specific emirates. In consideration to all the factors analyzed, the threat of new entries is relatively high.

5.2.5 Intensity of Rivalry among Competitors

In most industries, corporations are mutually dependent. A competitive move by one firm can be expected to have a noticeable effect on its competitors and thus may cause retaliation. A number of factors determine the intensity of rivalry: the number of competitors, industry growth rate, product and service characteristics, amount of fixed costs, capacity, high of exit barriers, and diversity of the rivals (Wheelen & Hunger, 2009).

Concentrated industries have lower rivalry than fragmented industries. The medical equipment imaging industry in the GCC and especially the medical imaging market is highly concentrated. High market growth rate indicates that more customers are entering the market, and as such competition is not based on capturing market share. Therefore, high market growth rates lower the intensity of the competition (Porter, 2008). The medical equipment market in GCC countries is growing at a higher rate than the global average (5% CAGR). In Saudi Arabia, the medical equipment market is expected to grow from US$479 million in 2008 to

US$672 million in 2013; this represents a 7% CAGR. The UAE's medical equipment market is expected to grow 6.4% CAGR from 2008-2013 (Business Monitor International, 2009). The diagnostic imaging equipment markets in KSA and UAE are expected to grow at a rate of 8% CAGR from 2008-2013 (Business Monitor International, 2009). Based on this factor, the intensity of the competition is relatively low.

The amount of fixed costs required, impact on the intensity of the competition; the higher the fixed costs, the higher the intensity of the competition (Wheelen & Hunger, 2009). Medical equipment providers bear high fixed costs associated with product research and development, technology production assets, and patent payments. Based on this factor, the level of competition is high. The cost that the customer bears when switching to another product or services has an impact on the intensity of the competition. Low switching costs make it easy for customers to switch to competing products, and thus increase the intensity of the competition required to retain market share. As mentioned earlier, switching costs tend to be high with variations occurring based on the nature of the purchase/ service contract.

If the perceived values offered by competitors' products are differentiated (unique), then the intensity of the competition decreases as customers opt for the product that best fits their specific needs. Competitors thus find it easier to retain their customers. As a high technology industry, competition in the medical equipment industry is based on continuous product innovations. In the GCC, medical imaging equipment providers are very similar; they compete vigorously in similar product lines and hold similar market share. Industries characterized by slow growth rates are highly competitive, as completion in slow growing industries is based on obtaining the competitor's market share. The medical equipment industry and the medical equipment market is growing at a slightly above average rate. In addition, competitors have very similar market shares. (ATKearney, 2008)

Exit barriers make it difficult or unattractive for companies to the leave the market, as a result they have to stay and intensify their competitive efforts to make a profit (Porter, 2008). High fixed costs in terms of manufacturing facilities (for

OEMs), as well as asset specificity (difficult to sell assets, when exiting), represent high exit barriers. Based on this factor, the intensity of the competition for OEMs is high. However, exit barriers are much lower for ISOs and small service providers, as they have substantially lower fixed assets. Considering all of the factors analyzed, competition in the market is high.

5.2.6 Porter's Five Forces Analysis Results

Table 16 below shows each force and its strength within the medical equipment industry:

Force	Strength
Threat of Substitutes	High
Bargaining Power of Buyers	Moderate
Bargaining Power of Suppliers	Moderate
Threat of New Entrants	High
Rivalry among Competitors	High

Table 15: Porter's Five Forces

According to Porter, the collective strength of the forces determines the ultimate profit potential in the industry. (Wheelen & Hunger, 2009) Collectively these forces within the medical equipment and services industry and the medical imaging market are moderate to high.

6. Healthcare in the UAE with focus on Abu Dhabi

Although healthcare industries in the GCC countries are very similar there are still some major variations. The scope of this dissertation was therefore concentrated on one of the most promising healthcare markets in the GCC: the United Arab Emirates (Statistics Centre - Abu Dhabi, 2011). Due to differences in legal regulation and economic approach, the scope of the study has been further focused on the Emirate of Abu Dhabi. The factors considered are used to evaluate the conceptual feasibility of the MES approach discussed. In order to obtain further intensive knowledge of the market and to verify the published data, a series of interviews were carried out with key professionals who have extensive experience in the GCC's healthcare industry. Among others, interviews were carried out with top senior regulatory officials in the UAE's health regulator bodies as well as with healthcare professionals working in premium healthcare facilities in the region. Interviews were also carried out with executives working in leading multinational MES providers, health consultancies, and radiology original equipment manufacturers. In addition, a survey (described later in this chapter) was conducted in order to understand the reality of operations within UAE's healthcare industry. While the survey respondents are based in the UAE and a number of interviewees are also based in the UAE, or gained most of their experience in UAE, the findings concluded from the results of both the interviews and the survey can still be applied to the rest of the GCC countries due to major similarities in their healthcare industries.

6.1 Leading Healthcare Authorities and Developments in UAE

The UAE's Government Strategy 2011-2013, has outlined the provision of world-class healthcare a priority (UAE CABINET, 2011). UAE's healthcare system comprises of 6,946 physicians (1.2 physicians per 1000 people) 13,936 nurses and midwives (WHO, 2010). In 2009, there were 12,868 (2 beds per 1000 people) hospital beds, 122 hospitals (54 of which are public hospitals) (Espicom Business Intelligence, 2010). By 2025, it is expected that growth in the demand for hospitals beds will increase by 160% (Mourshed, Hediger, & Lambert, 2007). According to the latest data released by the UAE Ministry of health, the UAE in 2007 had 915 clinics (Central Statistical Department, 2007). Medical tourism has substantially increased in the UAE and in order to promote this trend, hospital projects that will generate additional 9,000 hospital beds have been announced in 2009 (Alpen Capital Limited, 2009). The UAE Healthcare system consists of a comprehensive combination of private and public hospitals and associated regulatory bodies. Each entity has its own separate autonomous operation authorities which are run independently of each other (Rehman, 2008).

6.1.1 Ministry of Health (MoH)

The Ministry of Health is the ultimate healthcare authority in the UAE. It aims to provide preventive and curative healthcare to all the UAE's citizens through a network of primary secondary and clinical healthcare. According to the latest (2007) statistics released by the Ministry of Health, the MoH budget in 2007 was AED 1468.54 million amounting to AED490 per person (Central Statistical Department, 2007).

6.1.2 The Health Authority –Abu Dhabi (HAAD)

The Abu Dhabi Healthcare Authority is the highest state level regulatory body for Abu Dhabi's Healthcare Sector. The authority of the HAAD extends to the Abu Dhabi (city), Al Ain, as well as the Western and Eastern Districts of the UAE. HAAD is responsible for defining the strategy for its healthcare system, monitoring and assessing the health status of the population as well as the performance of the healthcare system. It is also responsible for the inspection and enforcement of healthcare standards in the regions for which it is responsible. The regulatory body has been engaged in promoting the awareness of lifestyle diseases (Health Authority, 2011).

6.1.3 Abu Dhabi Health Services Company (SEHA)

Abu Dhabi Healthcare Services Company (owned by the government of Abu Dhabi) that was established as part of Abu Dhabi's Healthcare Sector reform initiative, is an independent public joint stock company created to manage and develop the healthcare services of public hospitals and clinics in the Emirate of Abu

Dhabi. The company owns and runs 12 hospital facilities, 2,644 licensed beds, and more than 40 Ambulatory and Primary Healthcare Clinics (SEHA, 2009).

6.1.4 Dubai Health Authority (DHA)

Dubai Health Authority is Dubai's highest state level regulatory body. It is empowered to regulate and set the standards in all healthcare services in Dubai including all public, private, Free Zone and Ministry of Health facilities. DHA divides its services into four categories: hospital services, clinical support services, primary healthcare services, shared support services, and health policy and strategy (Government of Dubai, 2010). DHA services are provided in three main hospitals: Dubai Hospital, Rashid Hospital, and Al Wasl Hospital. The DHA's strategic goals focus on promoting private investment in Dubai's medical services, promoting transparency in the healthcare system (through implementing and setting healthcare information systems and standards), promoting a comprehensive healthcare funding policy (health insurance), and ensuring the supply of healthcare postgraduates (Government of Dubai, 2010).

6.1.5 Dubai Healthcare City (DHCC)

Dubai Healthcare City is a Free Zone in Dubai established to exclusively house healthcare facilities. DHCC contains 2 hospitals, 2000 medical professionals, and over 90 outpatient medical centres. Dubai Healthcare City is a TECOM investment (a subsidiary of government owned Dubai Holding) (DHCC, 2011). Healthcare services in DHCC are heavily regulated to guarantee the best healthcare service quality. According to Dubai Healthcare City LLC, "The Centre for Healthcare Planning and Quality (CPQ) was established jointly with Partners Harvard Medical International, as the independent regulatory body responsible for implementing rigorous standards that are aligned with international best practices to ensure the highest quality care." (DHCC, 2011)

6.2 Equipment Management in UAE

Due to a lack of comprehensive published data on the healthcare industry and the medical equipment market in the UAE, an online survey was conducted to acquire further information on the healthcare industry in general and on the medical equipment market in the UAE, in particular. The results of this survey as well as the relevant data attained from interviews with experts in the healthcare industry in the UAE will be used in this section to gain further insight into areas where there are currently information gaps.

The results of the survey used in this section are based on a sample of 30 respondents. The sample is composed of highly experienced individuals within the UAE's healthcare industry. In order to guarantee the validity of the data, survey respondents were first assessed to evaluate their level of experience in the market based on emails sent to these individuals.

Among the respondents, 41.9% of have more than eleven years of experience in the healthcare industry in the UAE, 13.3% have gained most of their experience in Abu Dhabi, and 70% have experiences in the other Emirates (mainly Dubai). Moreover, 38.7% of the respondents work at healthcare provision entities, 12.9% work in healthcare support services, 38.7% work at OEMs, and 6.5% work in other healthcare specialties. The profile also shows that 63% of the respondents have gained most of their experience working with government owned healthcare providers and 67.7% are highly involved in medical equipment management (MES Survey, 2011).

6.2.1 Equipment Planning in UAE

Medical equipment planning entails evaluating the medical facility's equipment and technology needs, evaluating existing equipment, deciding what additional equipment is required and what the equipment needs are (Wolper, 2004). The most important factors involved in equipment planning are performing a preliminary audit of existing equipment, assessing the compatibility of new technologies with the healthcare provider's current and future medical services, planning for selection and replacement of new technologies, setting priorities for technology acquisition, developing procedures for equipment procurement and monitoring how the equipment is being used (Bronzino, 2000).

According to an interview with a medical technology systems manufacturer, one of the main challenges faced with regards to equipment planning is evaluating and identifying the healthcare provider's equipment requirements and specifications (HC Consultancy 3, 2011). Rather than determining the right equipment for the medical facility, healthcare providers in the UAE tend to refer to equipment requirements and specifications of international healthcare providers. This statement had been further validated based on the survey results. Determining the healthcare provider's medical equipment requirements and specifications has been ranked as the most common difficulty with regards to medical equipment difficulty. (MES Survey, 2011)

Equipment budgeting and cost transparency & control have been identified as the 2nd and 3rd most common challenges. (HC Consultancy 1, 2011) According to Alpen Capital, "The majority of hospitals [in GCC] have no periodical budget or performance and efficiency targets. Moreover, many times, costs are simply not considered while deciding the purchase of equipment and other hospital utilities." (Alpen Capital Limited, 2009, S. 26) Medical equipment standardization was identified as the 4th most common problem based on the options given.

Planning for equipment selection and replacement in UAE is a process that generally varies based on the ownership structure of the healthcare provider. In government healthcare facilities, according to an interview conducted with the CEO of an Abu Dhabi based healthcare consultancy, the equipment selection and replacement process in the UAE is regulated by each Emirate's Health Authority (HC Consultancy 2, 2011). Equipment selection and replacement intentions also vary based on the ownership structure. According to the aforementioned interview, government hospitals want to raise the quality and standard of healthcare in the country and as such they opt for more advanced medical equipment. In contrast, according to the interview, while private sector players do care about the quality of the services provided, private healthcare providers are very profit-driven and will only purchase a piece of equipment if they think it will increase their profit margin. According to McKinsey, "The government has been offering incentives for private healthcare providers to increase the quality of healthcare. Based on the same report entitled, *Private Solutions for Health Care in the Gulf*, "To make sure that they're getting what they pay for, they [the Government] have already asked the private sector to provide a wider range and a higher quality of services…Some governments have helped private providers succeed, primarily by engaging them to manage public facilities and then reimbursing them for treating government-funded patients." (Mourshed, Hediger, & Lambert, 2007)

Based on the results, the most common cause leading to the replacement of medical equipment is continuous equipment malfunction. The 2nd and 3rd most common cause is the requirement for continuously more advanced equipment to compete, the need to change equipment due to its outdated status, respectively. Interviews with healthcare consultants have further validated this view (HC Consultancy 1, 2011) (HC Consultancy 3, 2011) (HC Consultancy 4, 2011). Equipment that is replaced in the UAE is sold, stored, or thrown away. Based on the survey, 25% of respondents reported that equipment is usually sold, and 21% revealed that the equipment is stored while the majority of the respondents (42.9%) responded that the equipment is thrown away (MES Survey, 2011). According to the interview with the CEO of the healthcare consultancy based in Abu Dhabi, the equipment in most cases is disposed off or stored and neglected. When equipment is outdated, as in most cases (78.6%), the equipment is replaced, only 25% of the respondents confirmed that the equipment is updated. According to the interview with the OEM service engineer, the majority of customers ask the OEM to replace the system. If the equipment can still be utilized, as in some cases, the equipment is given to the OEM who in exchange offers the healthcare provider a discount on the new system to be installed. The OEM then refurbishes the equipment and offers it for sale (OEM, 2011). As stated by 93% of the respondents, medical facilities would benefit from additional systematic and periodic equipment updates (MES Survey, 2011).

Part of the equipment planning process is identifying what additional equipment is needed. With respect to patient waiting time for therapeutic treatments, 66% of the respondents reported that waiting time is a problem in Abu Dhabi due to the insufficient number of therapeutic treatment devices available (MES Survey, 2011). According to *Abu Dhabi Health Statistics 2009*, waiting time for Oncology treatments has been classified as "Intermediate" (HAAD, 2009, p. 37).

Equipment planning also incorporates equipment monitoring. According to the survey results, equipment maintenance, service and repair, volume, and availability are recorded/ tracked. Very few respondents have confirmed that records are being kept on equipment usage and equipment operators (9.7% of confirmed), as well as on equipment spare parts and consumables (3.2% of confirmed) (MES Survey, 2011).

6.2.2 Equipment Procurement

Equipment procurement procedures in the UAE vary depending on the ownership structure of the healthcare provider. In public healthcare delivery facilities which constitute around 75% of the healthcare facilities in the UAE, the government allocates an equipment budget for each facility (Alpen Capital Limited, 2009). According to the interview conducted with the CEO of an Abu Dhabi based consultancy, in government facilities the doctor or physician is usually responsible for initiating the procurement process by establishing the need for new equipment. A series of specialized committees, the purchasing department, and biomedical engineers discuss the equipment requirements. The ultimate decision is made by the Emirate's corresponding health authority (this applies to large medical equipment). According to the results of the survey conducted, 22% of the respondents answered that the final purchase decision is made by the Health Authority and 64.3% answered that the equipment procurement process is initiated by the members of the department operating the equipment. Among the respondents, 63% based their answers on their experience working with government healthcare facilities (MES Survey, 2011). Large medical equipment in public healthcare facilities are bought through a tender process (OEM MES Provider, 2011) (Mourshed, Hediger, & Lambert, 2007).

The medical equipment procurement process followed by private healthcare facilities in the UAE varies. Based on the survey results and the interviews conducted, the procurement process is also initiated by the specialist in the department operating the equipment. The survey shows that 14.3% of the respondents pointed to the biomedical team as the entity that initiates the process (30% of the respondent have experience working with private healthcare providers). The final decision, according to both the survey and the interview conducted with multiple healthcare consultants is made either by the healthcare facility's board of directors or trustees. (25% of the respondents confirmed this) (HC Consultancy 2, 2011) (HC Consultancy 3, 2011).

With regards to the importance of equipment purchase decision factors, the survey shows that 75% of the respondents rated equipment specifications as very being "Very Important", 81.5% rated equipment maintenance and repair as being "Very Important", 70.4% rated equipment upgrade and replacement services as being "Very Important", 51.9% rated equipment flexibility as being very important and 70.4% rated equipment safety as being "Very Important" (MES Survey, 2011). The table below provides further details on the results of the survey pertaining to medical equipment purchase decisions factors.

	Very Unimportant	Unimportant	Somewhat Unimportant	Somewhat Important	Very Important	Not Applicable
Specifications	17.9%	0.0%	0.0%	7.1%	75.0%	0.0%
Price	11.1%	0.0%	0.0%	55.6%	33.3%	0.0%
Brand	7.4%	0.0%	3.7%	63.0%	25.9%	0.0%
Maintenance/ Repair services	14.8%	0.0%	3.7%	0.0%	81.5%	0.0%
Reliability	7.4%	0.0%	3.7%	18.5%	70.4%	0.0%
Upgrade/ Replacement services	3.7%	0.0%	7.4%	25.9%	63.0%	0.0%
Mobility	3.7%	3.7%	14.8%	66.7%	7.4%	3.7%
Flexibility	3.7%	3.7%	7.4%	33.3%	51.9%	0.0%
Level of Technology Advancement	3.7%	0.0%	0.0%	55.6%	40.7%	0.0%
Safety	7.4%	0.0%	3.7%	18.5	70.4%	0.0%
Customization	3.7%	3.7%	7.4%	77.8%	7.4%	0.0%
Automation	3.7%	3.7%	3.7%	85.2%	3.7%	0.0%

Table 16: Medical Equipment Procurement Decision Making Factors (MES Survey, 2011)

6.2.3 Equipment Training

Lack of training can lead to misdiagnosis and places both the healthcare provider and the patient at risk. (Peter R. Hoskins, 2010) According to the results of the survey, the most common cause for equipment related accidents/ injury has been attributed to lack of equipment safety and usage knowledge. The most common cause leading to errors when diagnosing diseases through medical imaging exams has been attributed to misinterpretation of the examination results. The second most common cause according to the survey is a lack of training and equipment knowledge. Medical equipment training in the UAE is mainly given to biomedical engineers and sometimes to doctors. In rare cases (if requested by the healthcare provider), medical equipment training is given to radiographers (OEM MES Provider, 2011).

According to 70% of the respondents, medical equipment training covers application usage training and only 11% of respondents answered that medical equipment training is extended to hardware usage. According to 59% of the respondents, training for complex medical equipment usually lasts for a period of one session and then periodic refresher sessions are given. Furthermore, 30% of the respondents answered that training is given once and 92.6% of the respondents confirmed that they think that periodic refresher sessions would be beneficial. According to the interview with the OEM Service engineer, an applications specialist provides training through a one- time session. If the equipment is complex, initial training is carried out, and after an appropriate period of time, a second training session is given. Accordingly, 52% of the respondents replied that they are satisfied with the equipment training that was carried out, 11% were very satisfied and 15% of the respondents were dissatisfied with the medical equipment training that is given (MES Survey, 2011).

6.2.4 Equipment Maintenance & Repair

Predominantly medical equipment maintenance and repair in the UAE is conducted via an external source (according to 59.3% of the respondents). Only 25.9% of the respondents confirmed that equipment maintenance and repair is conducted both by the healthcare providers' dedicated staff (internally) and by an external source. Internal maintenance and repair according to 75% of the respondents is done by the biomedical engineering team while 7% of the respondents replied that medical equipment maintenance is done via a dedicated internal maintenance team. In the survey, 53.3% of the respondents answered that those who conduct internal maintenance and repair are sometimes capable of solving the problem, 20% answered that they are always capable of solving the problem, and 13.3% answered that they are never capable of solving the problem. In terms of satisfaction, 20% of the respondents answered that they were very satisfied with the response time of the healthcare provider's dedicated internal maintenance and repair staff. With regards to the overall quality of internal maintenance and repair, 33.3% of the respondents are somewhat satisfied, 20% are satisfied, and 13.3% are very satisfied. Based on the transparency of the internal maintenance and repair cost, 28% of the respondents answered that there are hidden costs associated with internal maintenance and repair. 33.3% replied that the costs were associated with internal maintenance and repair (MES Survey, 2011).

External maintenance in the UAE according to 84% of the respondents is done by the OEM's maintenance and repair team and 12% replied that it is conducted via the equipment's independent service provider team. The results also showed that 68% of the respondents replied that the external team is always cable of solving the problem and 24% replied that the external team is capable of solving the problem most of the time. In terms of satisfaction, 16% of the respondents are very satisfied with the response time of the external maintenance and repair team, 48% were just satisfied and 24% were sometimes satisfied. Based on the overall quality of the external maintenance and repair services, 16.7% were very satisfied, 50% were satisfied and 4.2% were somewhat dissatisfied. In terms of transparency, 28% of the respondents answered that there are hidden costs associated with external maintenance and repair, and 56% answered that there are none.

While the majority of the respondents have not heard of MES, according to the research results, 64.7% of the respondents answered that non-core professional responsibilities are restricting professionals from focusing on their core professional responsibilities.

6.3 Overview of Healthcare in Abu Dhabi

To be able to evaluate the possibilities of an MES approach in Abu Dhabi, the Abu Dhabi Healthcare market was analyzed in this section.

6.3.1 Healthcare Indicators

Abu Dhabi is the capital of UAE as well as its largest Emirate. The latest statistics available indicate that Abu Dhabi contributes to 55% of the UAE's GDP (Bitar, 2009). 2009 estimates indicate that Abu Dhabi generates a GDP of AED 546,476 million (US$149,719 million).This amounts to a GDP per capita of AED 332,500 (US$91,095.8), one of the world's highest GDP per capita, and the highest GDP per capita in UAE (Statistics Centre - Abu Dhabi, 2011) (CIA, 2011). 0.4% of Abu Dhabi's GDP is dedicated to health; this amounts to AED 2,106 million (US$576.9 million) (Statistics Centre - Abu Dhabi, 2011). Health expenditure as percentage of GDP is expected to grow by 7.8% according to 2009 estimates. Abu Dhabi houses a population of 1.9 million, 21% of whom are nationals. Two third of the population living in the Emirate are under the age of 30 (Central Statistical Department, 2009). Abu Dhabi's healthcare network consists of 5,142 physicians, 8,142 nurses and 5,630 allied health professionals in 1,077 licensed facilities. There are 39 hospitals in Abu Dhabi (contributing to a total of 3,631 beds), 572 centres and clinics, and 467 pharmacies and stores (Central Statistical Department, 2009). Based on HAAD statistics, Table 18 in the next page presents the most significant health related indicators for 2009. The number of physicians per 1000 population in Abu Dhabi is the highest in GCC, the number of beds/ 100 patients however, is the lowest in the GCC countries.

Life expectancy at birth (2008), male	74.4
Life expectancy at birth (2008), female	74.8
Crude birth rate/ 1000	15.2
Crude death rate/ 1000	1.6
Leading causes of death (rate /10,000)	
Cardiovascular diseases	37.9
Injuries and poisoning	36.8
Cancer	20.8
Congenital anomalies	10.8
Diabetes Mellitus	10.8
Healthcare Facilities/ Resources	
Bed/ 1000	3.0
Doctor/ 1000	2.3
Nurse/ 1000	4.2

Table 17: Abu Dhabi Health Indicators (Chan, Medical Technology Management Practice, 2003)

In 2007, health insurance was made mandatory for all expatriate residents in the UAE and Thiqa was introduced for Nationals. Thiqa, managed by Damam (a national health insurance company) provides comprehensive health coverage to UAE nationals exclusively (Daman, 2011). In 2009, there were 33 insurance companies which processed 9.1 million insurance claims, 98.8% of which were for outpatient services. Due to the mandatory health insurance and Thiqa, the demand for healthcare services in the UAE has significantly increased. In 2009, there were more than 2.3 million health insurance contracts in Abu Dhabi; since this number is larger than the population of Abu Dhabi, it indicates, that a significant number of the population has multiple health insurance contracts. (Daman, 2011) These figures are indicative of the growth in healthcare demand. According to HAAD, there will be significant growth in demand for healthcare services related to chronic diseases, cardiovascular diseases, cancer, and diabetes mellitus. This will therefore stimulate growth in demand for outpatient services. The next Table provides outpatient and in-patient demand for 2009 and demand growth projections for 2019 (Chan, 2003).

				Additional Capacity Needed Over Ten Years							
	Current 2019			CAGR		Absolute		Annualized			
	2009	Low	High	Low	High	Low	High	Low	High		
Outpatients (m)	10	16	22	4.7	7.5	6	11	0.5	0.8	Including Churn	
Inpatient (000's)	180	237	312	2.8	5.7	57	132	5	10		
Beds	3,500	4,600	6000	2.5	5.4	1,000	2,400	90	190	High	Low
Doctors	5,300	8,200	10,700	4.4	7.3	2,900	5,400	230	390	1,300	1,700
Nurses	6,900	10,600	13,900	4.4	7.3	3,700	7,000	300	500	1,400	1,900

Table 18: Capacity Demand Projections (HAAD, 2009)

The table above indicates that there will be a minimum of 4.7% CAGR until 2019. There will also be an increase in demand for in-patient services. Both an increase in demand for in-patient and outpatient services will stimulate a demand for more doctors, nurses, and hospital beds. By 2019 at the very least, 4600 hospital beds, 8,200 doctors, and 10,600 additional nurses will be required. The addition of 4,200 beds was planned in 2010, 1,782 of which will be added by 2011 (HAAD, 2009).

The current capacity gaps and demand projections indicate that there may be a need for a business such as MES that could help the healthcare sector deal with the added demand for healthcare services.

6.3.2 Healthcare Ownership Structures in Abu Dhabi

In Abu Dhabi two stakeholders are involved, the independent MES provider and the government of Abu Dhabi. The information below has been obtained from multiple interviews with healthcare professionals working in Abu Dhabi. Healthcare providers can be classified into four major categories: publicly managed hospitals, privately managed hospitals, co-managed hospitals (PPPs) and charity hospitals.

- **Publicly Managed Hospitals**

  Publicly managed hospitals are run completely by the government of Abu

Dhabi. Public hospitals typically have large capacities since citizens across all socio-economic classes go to public hospitals for treatment. Publicly managed hospitals are completely funded by the government and are cash rich. Equipment purchasing occurs through a tender process.

- **Privately managed hospitals**
  Private hospitals are completely managed by individual private entities. These hospitals usually have small to medium capacities. In most cases these hospitals are run by a doctor(s), who is/ are also the owner(s), and as such they can be at times, low on funds. Thus financing equipment can be problematic. As far as purchase of medical equipment is considered, it is the owner of the hospital who makes the choice of a vendor.

- **Co-managed hospitals**
  Co-managed hospitals works under a public-private partnership between the government who own the setup and the private entities that are responsible for managing the clinical and non-clinical operations. In the emirate of Abu Dhabi, the government set up Abu Dhabi Health Services company that owns about 10-12 hospitals in the emirate. All these hospitals are managed privately by world renowned bodies in the healthcare sector. Co-managed hospitals are generally medium to large in size. These hospitals showcase state of the art medical equipment. Medical equipment purchasing is also based on tenders. The stakeholders in the decision making process are the biomedical engineers, the radiology department, and the Health Authority of Abu Dhabi. The hospital is expected to fund a certain percentage of equipment purchase from its own revenues.

- **Charity Hospitals**
  Charity hospitals are funded by charities and are operated by trusts. These hospitals are normally medium to large in bed capacity. Since the nature of funds received from charity is always variable, charity hospitals are very often low on funds.

6.3.3 MES Potential: Radiology Equipment in Abu Dhabi

Based on Abu Dhabi's GDP contribution to the UAE's GDP, an idea can be obtained about the size of Abu Dhabi's medical and diagnostic imaging equipment markets. Abu Dhabi's health and social work sectors account for 4% of the Emirate's US$149,719 million GDP (SCAD, 2011) (SCAD, 2011). Abu Dhabi's economic activities contribute to 55% of the UAE's GDP of US$224.9 billion, US$5.8 billion of which is spent on health (Bitar, 2009) (Espicom Business Intelligence, 2010). According to data collected from the Abu Dhabi Department of Health, Economist Intelligence, and Episcom, the UAE's medical device market in 2009 was worth US$641 million (approximately 10% of total health expenditures) (HAAD, 2009) (Espicom Business Intelligence, 2010).

This figure according to the sources previously mentioned, is forecasted to grow to US$819 million by 2014 (8.4% of total health expenditure). Business Monitor International estimates indicate that from 2008-2013, the UAE's medical device market will expand by a rate of 6.2%, thereby exceeding the global average rate of 5% (Espicom Business Intelligence, 2010). This expansion is due to an increased demand for high-tech medical equipment. Due to the rising expense in healthcare, healthcare authorities are expected to be more frugal in searching for the best price possible. As a result, according to BMI, medical device expenditure as a percentage of total health expenditures is expected to fall from 6.5% in 2008 to 5.3% in 2013. In 2009 the diagnostic imaging apparatus market[16] was worth US$146.3 million dollars (roughly 23% of the total value of UAE's medical device market) and is expected to grow to US$203 million dollars by 2014. (Espicom Business Intelligence, 2009)

Thus it could be assumed that an equivalent increase in the demand for radiology services is to be expected. The graph below derived from Episcom UAE Medisat Outlook 2009 provides projections for the sizes of the electro-diagnostic and x-ray apparatus markets.

[16] This includes only electrodiagnostic apparatus and X-ray apparatus.

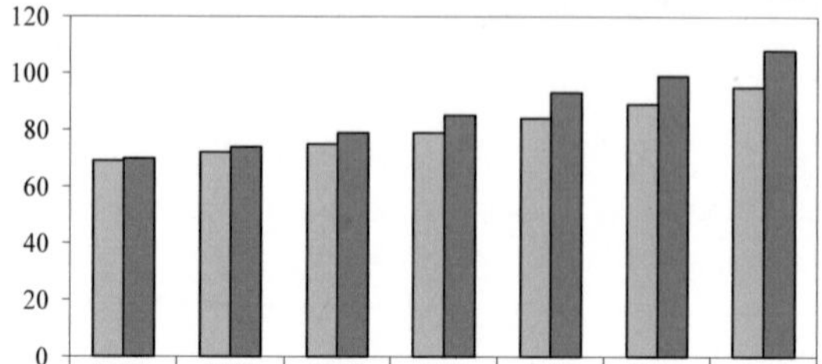

	2008	2009	2010	2011	2012	2013	2014
Electrodiagnostic	69	72	75	79	84	89	95
X-ray apparatus	70	74	79	85	93	99	108

Figure 17: UAE Electro-Diagnostic and X-ray Apparatus Market, 2008-2014 (Espicom Business Intelligence, 2009)

Current demand for radiology services is high. Considering that Abu Dhabi is one of the largest medical markets in the UAE, it could be assumed that the trends and patterns applicable to the UAE's health sector and medical equipment market and radiology services as a whole (mentioned in the previous paragraph) are also applicable to that of Abu Dhabi. Thus, the projected increase in need for radiology, represented through an increase in need for diagnostic imaging equipment in the UAE as a whole, aforementioned in the previous paragraph, could also be expected in Abu Dhabi. This can be proved further through specific health trends that are occurring in Abu Dhabi. In 2009, 9.1 million insurance claims were processed in Abu Dhabi, 98.8% of which were for outpatient procedures (HAAD, 2009). Outpatient services are defined as healthcare services that are not provided on the basis of an overnight stay in a room and board costs are incurred. Outpatient services are largely services that relate to diagnosis (e.g. lab tests and MRI scans), therapeutic services and treatments (e.g. some surgical procedures and chemotherapy), and rehabilitation (e.g. physical therapy) (Shi & Singh, 2008). It is predicted that there will be a further increase in outpatient services due to a significant growth in demand for services related to chronic diseases. The most prevalent chronic diseases are cardiovascular diseases such as hypertension, diabetes, high cholesterol. Chronic diseases are also related to respiratory diseases (due to the prevalence of smoking), and obesity complications, most of which are cardiovascular complications. One third of the population of the Emirates are overweight, of whom, 36% are obese. Among nationals, 17% have high blood pressure. Demand for in-patient treatment will also increase due to a projected increase in demand for cancer and diabetes treatments. Cancer in 2009 accounted for 14% of deaths in Abu Dhabi. Breast cancer, detected primarily through a mammography scan, is the most prevalent type of cancer in Abu Dhabi. By 2025 it is expected that diabetes will affect 25% of the population of the UAE as a whole. (HAAD, 2009)

In 2009, 77.7% of treatment value was dedicated to outpatient treatment. Services constituted 27.7% of outpatient value; procedures were worth 47.1%, drugs were worth 23.9%, and supplies were worth 1.3%. 22.3% of revenue went towards in-patient treatments. Services were worth 40.6% of total in-patient value; procedures were worth 50.6%, drugs were worth 5.8%, and supplies were worth 3.0% (HAAD, 2009). Disease conditions with the highest value in terms in-patient and outpatient treatment services, procedures, drugs, and supplies in order of the highest value are: cardiovascular diseases, respiratory infections, endocrine disorders. (HAAD, 2009) As derived from the Abu Dhabi Health Authority, the next tables (Table 20 and Table 21) provide a detailed breakdown of the value of each disease based on in-patient and outpatient procedures services and supplies.

	Total Inpatient and Outpatient	Outpatient (77.70%)				
		Volume	Services	Procedures	Drugs	Supplies
% of Total Value	100	100	27.7	47.1	23.9	1.3
Non-disease conditions	18.7	18.5	4.7	10.8	2.7	
Cardiovascular disease	8.7	8.8	2.3	3.1	3.2	0.2
Respiratory Infections	7.8	8.4	3.1	2.6	2.6	
Endocrine Disease	6.4	6.6	1.4	2.8	2.3	
Musculoskeletal Diseases	6.3	6.4	1.7	3	1.6	
Digestive Diseases	6.2	5.8	1.7	2.5	1.6	
Maternal and Perinatal	6.2	4.7	2.2	2.3	0.2	

Conditions						
Oral Conditions	6.2	7.5	1.2	6	1.3	
Gentourinary Diseases	5.6	5.2	1.4	2.7	1	
Diabetes Mellitus	5.4	5.9	1.3	1.8	2.7	
Respiratory Disease	4.6	4.2	1.3	1.5	1.4	
Infectious Parasitic dis-eases	3.3	3.5	1.1	1.5	0.8	
Skin Diseases	3.2	3.6	1.2	1.4	1	
Sense Organ Diseases	3.2	3.3	1.2	1.4	0.6	
Neuropsychiatric Condi-tions	2.7	2.7	0.7	1.1	0.8	
Cancer	1.9	1.5	0.4	0.7	0.4	
Nutritional Deficiencies	1.8	2	0.4	1.1	0.5	
Injuries	0.7	0.6		0.3		
Congenital Abnormalities	0.7	0.5		0.3		
RTA	0.2					

Table 19: Encounters by Diagnosis Group, % of value (Outpatient) (HAAD, 2009)

	Total Inpatient and Outpatient	Inpatient (22.30%)				
		Volume	Services	Procedures	Drugs	Supplies
% of Total Value	100	100	40.6	50.6	5.8	3
Non-disease conditions	18.7	19.3	7.4	10.5	0.8	0.5
Cardiovascular disease	8.7	8.3	3.9	3.6	0.4	0.4
Respiratory Infections	7.8	5.7	2.6	2.6	0.3	
Endocrine Disease	6.4	5.8	1.8	3.0	0.5	0.6
Musculoskeletal Diseases	6.3	5.9	2.8	2.8		0.2
Digestive Diseases	6.2	7.5	3.5	3.5	0.4	
Maternal and Perinatal Conditions	6.2	11.4	4.1	7.0	0.2	
Oral Conditions	6.2	1.4	0.4	0.8		
Gentourinary Diseases	5.6	7.1	2.9	3.0	1	
Diabetes Mellitus	5.4	3.6	1.3	1.9	0.2	
Respiratory Disease	4.6	6.2	2.3	3.3	0.3	
Infectious Parasitic diseases	3.3	2.8	1.2	1.3	0.2	
Skin Diseases	3.2	2.2	0.9	1.1		
Sense Organ Diseases	3.2	2.9	1.1	1.5		
Neuropsychiatric Conditions	2.7	2.8	1.4	1.1		
Cancer	1.9	3.2	1.5	1.4	0.3	
Nutritional Deficiencies	1.8	1.1	0.4	0.6		
Injuries	0.7	1.2	0.4	0.7		
Congenital Abnormalities	0.7	1.4	0.6	0.7		
RTA	0.2	0.4				

Table 20: Encounters by Diagnosis Group, % of value (Inpatient) (HAAD, 2009)

Some of the most prevalent and most expensive outpatient procedures involve radiology equipment for both the diagnosis and the treatment of diseases. An echo-exam is among the most valuable outpatient diagnostic procedures for cardiovascular disease; x-rays are prevalently used in detecting respiratory diseases and MRI's are used for musculoskeletal disease, ultrasound exams are used for digestive diseases and for viewing the fetus, PET scans, mammography scans, and CT scans are used in detecting cancer. In terms of in-patient procedures, angiography is among the most valuable procedures for cardiovascular diseases. (Mourshed, Hediger, & Lambert, 2007). Radiology equipment is also required for the treatment of cancer.

Diagnosis group	Overall	Top 5*	1st	2nd	3rd	4th	5th
Non-disease conditions	21.6	12.7	Complete CBC With Auto Diff WBC	Vaginal Delivery Only	OB US >/= 14 wks, Singl Fetus	Echo Exam Of Heart	Us Exam, Abdom, Complete
Maternal and Perinatal conditions	7.2	58.5	Vaginal Delivery Only	C Delivery Only	Vaginal Delivery Postpartum Care	OB US >/= 14 wks, Singl Fetus	C Delivery Only W/Postartum Care
Cardiovascular diseases	7.2	17.0	Echo Exam Of Heart	Lipid Panel	Glycosylated Hemoglobin Test	Cath Placement, Angiography	Left Heart Catheterization
Musculoskeletal diseases	7.0	16.7	MRI Lumbar Spine w/o Dye	Knee Arthroscopy/Surgery	MRI Joint Of lwr Extrem w/o Dye	MRI Neck Spine w/o Dye	Complete CBC With Auto Diff WBC
Digestive diseases	6.7	16.8	Ther/Proph/Diag Inj, iv Push	US Exam, Abdom, Complete	Upper GI Endoscopy, Biopsy	Laparoscopic Cholecystectomy	Complete CBC With Auto Diff WBC
Endocrine disorders	6.7	19.1	Gastroplasty w/o V-Band	Lipid Panel	Free Assay (Ft-3)	Assay Of Serum Albumin	Glycosylated Hemoglobin Test
Genitourinary diseases	6.5	16.2	US Exam, Pelvic, Complete	Transvaginal US, Non-OB	US Exam, Abdom, Complete	US Exam Abdo Back Wall, Comp	Complete CBC With Auto Diff WBC
Diabetes mellitus	6.0	24.9	Lipid Panel	Glycosylated Hemoglobin Test	Assay Of Serum Albumin	Hepatic Function Panel	Assay, Glucose, Blood Quant
Oral conditions	6.0	25.5	Installment For Treatment In Progress	Crown, Porcelain/Ceranic/Polymer Glass + L	Appliance, Maxillary + L	Three Canals	Two Surfaces
Respiratory infections	5.9	9.3	Complete CBC With Auto Diff WBC	Nasal Endoscopy, dx	Ther/Proph/Diag Inj, sc/im	Airway Inhalation Treatment	Chest X-Ray
Respiratory diseases	3.5	20.5	Repair Of Nasal Septum	Remove Tonsils And Adenoids	Nasal Endoscopy, dx	CT Maxillofacial w/o Dye	Airway Inhalation Treatment
Skin diseases	3.2	11.4	Complete CBC With Auto Diff WBC	Ther/Proph/Diag Inj, iv Push	Drainage Of Skin Abscess	Drainage Of Skin Abscess	Hepatic Function Panel
Sense organ diseases	3.0	16.9	Cataract Surg W/Iol, 1 Stage	Remove Impacted Ear Wax	Revision Of Cornea	Drain External Ear Lesion	Treatment Of Retinal Lesion
Infectious and parasitic diseases	3.0	14.6	Destruct B9 Lesion, 1-14	US Exam, Pelvic, Complete	Complete CBC With Auto Diff WBC	Transvaginal US, Non-OB	US Exam, Abdom, Complete
Neuropsychiatric conditions	2.0	22.5	Medication Management	Psytx, Off, 20-30 Min W/E&M	MRI Brain w/o Dye	Psytx, Hosp, 20-30 Min W/E&M	Complete CBC With Auto Diff WBC
Nutritional deficiencies	2.0	19.9	Free Assay (Ft-3)	Assay Of Parathormone	Assay Of Serum Albumin	Assay Of Vitamin D	Lipid Panel
Cancer	1.5	17.0	Chemo, iv Infussion, 1 hr	Total Hysterectomy	Pet Image w/CT, Full Body	Partial Removal Of Kidney	THER/PROPH/DIAG IV INF, INIT
Injuries	0.5	20.3	Ther/Proph/Diag Inj, sc/im	Repair Superficial Wound(S)	Immunohistochemistry	Dressing Change Not For Burn	Hydration iv Infussion, Init
Congenital anomalies	0.5	12.4	Echo Exam Of Heart	Echo Transthoracic	Transcath iv Stent, Percut	Complete CBC With Auto Diff WBC	Pet Image w/CT, Full Body
RTA	0.1	43.5	Ther/Proph/Diag Inj, iv Push	Ther/Prop/Diag Inj/Inf Proc	Ther/Proph/Dg Iv Inf, Add-On	Assay Of Serum Albumin	Ther/Proph/Diag Inj, Sc/Im

Table 21: Top Procedures by Value and Diagnosis Group (HAAD, 2009)

The table above provides a breakdown on the top procedures performed for each disease category based on the procedure's value. Currently, the largest capacity gaps are evident in the provision of most medical specialties as shown in the following table. This provides high potential for future growth. The current capacity gaps and projected increase in demand for treatment of specific chronic diseases (diabetes, and cardiovascular disease), lifestyle diseases (obesity) and cancer, call for the establishment of more super-specialty centres with state-of-the art facilities as well as the construction of additional medical centres (Mourshed, Hediger, & Lambert, 2007).

Specialty	Facilities	Staff	No. Physicians	Walk-in	For appointment
Internal medicine	⇧	⇧	194	✓ <1 hour	! 2-3 days
*Obstetrics & Gynecology	⇧	⇧	222	✗ 2-3 hours	✗ - 5-6 days
Ophthalmology	⇧	⇧	106	! 1-2 hours	! - 2-3 days
Orthopedics	⇧	⇧	120	✗ 2-3 hours	! - 2-3 days
Pediatric surgery	⇧	⇧	22	! 1-2 hours	✓ - 1-2 days
Pediatrics	⇧	⇧	326	! 1-2 hours	✓ - 1-2 days
Rheumatology	⇧	⇧	15	! 1-2 hours	! - 2-4 days
Intensive & Critical care medicine	⇧	⇧	39	n/a	n/a
Psychiatry	⇧	⇧	31	✗ 2-3 hours	! - 2-3 days
Neonatology	⇧	⇧		✓ <1 hour	! 2-3 days
Gastroenterology	⇧	⬈	29	! + 1-2 hours	✗ - 5-6 days
Urology	⬈	⇧	70	! 1-2 hours	! - 2-4 days
Endocrinology	⬈	⬈	32	! - 1-2 hours	✗ 1-2 weeks
General medicine	⬈	⬈	9	! 1-2 hours	✓ no appt
Nephrology	⬈	⬈	32	✓ <1 hour	! - 4-5 days
Oncology	⬈	⬈	17	! 1-2 hours	! - 3-5 days
Otolaryngology (ENT)	⬈	⬈	113	✗ 2-3 hours	! 2-3 days
Physical medicine & Rehabilitation	⬈	⬈	9	n/a	✓ 1 day
Dentistry	⬈	⬈	754	! 1-2 hours	! 2-3 days
General surgery	⬈	⬊	212	! 1-2 hours	! 5 days
Pulmonology	⬈	⬊	17	n/a	n/a
Allergy & Immunology	⬊	⇧	2	✓ 1 hour	✓ - 1 day
Cardiology	⬊	⇧	80	! + 1-2 hours	✓ - 2 days
Dermatology	⬊	⇧	121	! + 1-2 hours	✓ - 2 days
Emergency medicine	⬊	⇧	117	✓ 10-15 minutes	✓ no appt
Preventive medicine	⬊	⇧		n/a	n/a
Hematology	⬊	⬈	8	✓ 20-30 minutes	✓ 1 day
Nuclear medicine	⬊	⬈	7	n/a	! + 1-7 days
Oral & Maxillofacial surgery	⬊	⬈	9	! 1-2 hours	✗ - 5-6 days
Radiology	⬊	⬈	115	✓ <1 hour	✓ - 1-2 days
**Family medicine	⬊	⬈	1,579	! 1-2 hours	! 3-5 days
Neurology	⬊	⬊	24	! 1-2 hours	! - 4-5 days
Cardio-thoracic surgery	⬊	⬊	24	n/a	n/a
Infectious diseases	⬊	⬊	8	n/a	n/a
Alternative therapies	⬊	⬊	36	✓ 10-20 minutes	✓ 1 day
Anesthesiology	⇩	⬈	177	n/a	n/a
Pathology	⇩	⬊	112	n/a	n/a

How does capacity need to change?
- ⇧ Clearly more
- ⬈ Somewhat more
- ⬊ About right or somehwat fewer
- ⇩ Clearly fewer

Waiting times
- ✓ Low
- ! Intermediate
- ✗ High
- + Longer than 2008
- - Shorter than 2008

Table 22: Current Capacity Gaps (HAAD, 2009)

Due to a predicted increase in the number of medical facilities and an increase in the capacity of existing facilities, it can be assumed that there will be an equivalent increase in the demand for medical equipment. Thus an MES program might be required to manage the burden of large medical equipment inventory in Abu Dhabi's medical facilities. An increase in the number of people with cardiovascular diseases, respiratory diseases, diabetes, and cancer and the current matching capacity gaps will lead to an increase in demand for radiology equipment required to diagnose and treat these diseases (Mourshed, Hediger, & Lambert, 2007). As mentioned in the *MES Healthcare Market Opportunities in GCC* section of this report, it is expected that the GCC governments will engage private players through outsourcing specific aspects of facility management. Sheikh Khalifa Medical City (managed by Cleveland Clinic), Tawam Hospital, and Tawam Molecular Imaging Centre (both are managed by Johns Hopkins Medicine International) are three examples of medical facilities that are managed by private entities in Abu Dhabi (Johns Hopkins Medicine International, 2010). Tawam Molecular Imaging Centre and Tawam Hospital are both owned by Mubadala Development Company (Abu Dhabi Government's investment arm) (Johns Hopkins Medicine International, 2010). Mubadala also hired German medical solutions provider Siemens to design, build, and partly operate a specialist molecular imaging centre for Tawam Hospital. Siemens provided the hospital with a PET CT diagnostic system and a Cyclotron radioisotope delivery system (Staff Report Mubadala, 2007).

6.3.4 Dominant Radiology Equipment Providers in UAE and Abu Dhabi

UAE imports 88% of its medical equipment; in 2009 medical equipment imports were worth US$1.5 billion (Espicom Business Intelligence, 2010). This equipment is mainly imported from Italy, France, Germany, US, UK, Sweden, Japan and China. The leading importers of diagnostic medical imaging equipment are General Electric (GE), Philips Medical Systems and Siemens Healthcare. These companies all compete vigorously in similar product lines. GE has the highest market share in diagnostic imaging equipment and overall radiology equipment. In radiotherapy, Elekta / Philips has the highest market share. In litho trip, Dornier and Siemens are major market share holders. As for patient monitoring equipment, GE/ Marquette dominates the market; major players include Space Labs and HP. In endoscopy, American companies lead the market for rigid endoscopes used in invasive surgery. In diagnostic Ear, Nose, and Thorax (ENT) endoscopy, German companies lead the market (National Institute for Foreign Trade, 2011).

7. Recommendation, Outlook and Conclusion

Conceptually, this dissertation evaluated whether MES, particularly for radiology equipment, would add value to the welfare of the healthcare industry in the GCC region. In order to investigate the viability of MES in the GCC, the United Arab Emirates was chosen as a representative country for the GCC region upon which the intensity and focus of evaluation was concentrated on. As such, the healthcare industry in the UAE was assessed. Due to the variations between the healthcare industries of each Emirate in the UAE, the evaluation especially focused on Abu Dhabi. As previously stated and explained, Abu Dhabi as the capital was chosen due to its strong economic standing, reformed healthcare regulatory framework as well as specific health demographic and psychographic factors. Theoretical models were developed for MES from a more global perspective taking into consideration their adaptability to the GCC region. Based on the scope of the evaluation (GCC with a focus on UAE/Abu Dhabi), this chapter took into consideration all of the information integrated into this dissertation and accordingly provided recommendations that are meant to raise the quality of healthcare in the GCC region through MES. An outlook into the healthcare industry that identifies areas of opportunity for the development of the healthcare industry in the GCC is then described. An overall summary of the main findings of this dissertation is hereby given.

7.1 Recommendations

The continuous innovation and advancement of medical equipment has greatly contributed to the quality of health and life. Innovation and advancement of medical technology however has negative repercussions; the innovation cycle generates equipment that is complex, costly, and requires intensive equipment knowledge. Due to the speed of the development and replacement cycle of radiology equipment and associated technology, the process of equipment planning, procurement, training and implementation requires substantial insight, time and financial resources. (Hanna, 2001) Globally and regionally, the cost of equipment ownership as well as the complete life-cycle cost of equipment is not considered resulting in unrepresentative budgets and misleading equipment planning decisions thereby leading to inefficient and ineffective equipment purchases. (Alpen Capital Limited, 2009) (David & Judd, 2000, pp. 168-11) This reduces the ability of healthcare providers in the GCC region to the knowledge of product life-cycle costs of advanced equipment that have long shelf lives and requires extensive experience and knowledge. MES program's offerings would provide the required experience that enables healthcare providers in the GCC region to make sound decisions. Radiology equipment is especially critical and thus it is essential that uptime is guaranteed. (Dolan, 2004) Through both extending the lifetime of medical equipment through sound maintenance and equipment care services, as well as by contributing to more effective and efficient healthcare management practices, MES can raise the quality of healthcare in the region. (Sallas, Lane, Mathews, Watkins, & Wiley-Patton, 2007)

There have been dramatic challenges in the healthcare market and the demographic profile of the GCC region; these developments have created new areas for business opportunities. Specifically, there is a gap in the delivery field of radiology and associated services. Population growth, new health risk factors, and expanding aging populations have created opportunities for growth in healthcare delivery. (Mourshed, Hediger, & Lambert, 2007) Based on the disease demand profile and the surge in chronic diseases and cancer, it is predicted that there will be high demand for radiology equipment that are required to diagnose and treat these diseases (HAAD, 2009).

Radiology OEMs currently dominate the radiology equipment and services markets. Due to a lack of healthcare management experience and knowledge, it has been concluded that an independent view is required to provide these management services.[17] In this regard, the GCC region, more specifically the UAE, is lacking. There are very few large independent service providers in the UAE; the UAE market is monopolistic in the sense that there is only one distributor who sells a specific product or service brand. (National Institute for Foreign Trade,

17 It was concluded, as mentioned under the *Equipment Management in UAE* section, that OEMs dominate the UAE market based on the results of the Managed Equipment Services in UAE survey. 84% of the respondents answered that the OEM provides equipment maintenance and repair services. Only 12% answered that the independent vendor provides equipment maintenance and repair services.

2011) Based on the analysis of the threat of substitutes (for OEMs), the threat of substitutes for independent service providers is high. This indicates that there is success potential for an MES program provided by an independent service provider. Alternatively, the MES provider as an independent service provider can work with all of the OEMs in the market and thus share rather than take away market share. (MES Survey, 2011)

The analysis concluded that there is a market gap in independent imaging equipment service providers in the GCC. This demonstrates a barrier to enter the market but could be surrounded by a potential MES approach with partnering with multiple existing OEMs to gain market share. (MES Survey, 2011)

The services provided through an MES program match the current needs of healthcare providers in the GCC and more specifically in UAE. Strategic alliance and management, equipment planning, implementation, ongoing user training and disposal offer a lot of possibilities for healthcare providers in the GCC. The strategic alliance and management service is especially important because public healthcare providers in the region lack healthcare management and regulation experience (Alpen Capital Limited, 2009). In addition, the equipment replacement service allows both the MES provider and the healthcare provider to profit and achieve cost savings. Using its current customer base, the MES provider could take the old equipment from one customer, refurbish it and then sell it to another customer that does not require advanced equipment in the region or in other countries. Research university hospitals require the most advanced equipment to conduct research; as such they rapidly change their medical equipment inventory. Equipment from such hospitals can easily be refurbished and resold. (OEM, 2011) The healthcare provider benefits by getting a discount and the MES provider benefits by generating additional profits from used inventory. Healthcare providers can also achieve cost savings through buying large volumes of equipment from the MES provider if the MES provider offers a sales volume discount. (OEM, 2011)

An MES program would thus be beneficial due to the rising cost of healthcare in the region and the recent increase in the price sensitivity of payers. (Mourshed,

Hediger, & Lambert, 2007) Since the cost of equipment services and procurement is passed off to the patient, the payer also benefits by reduction in price of healthcare treatments (HC Consultancy 2, 2011). By implementing an MES program in the GCC countries, overall synergies can be created and established between all the stake holders involved, leading to a decrease in the cost of healthcare and an increase in the quality of healthcare.

By outsourcing specific equipment management and maintenance activities, the healthcare provider reduces internal responsibilities allowing the provider to effectively and efficiently perform core business processes (Chan, 2003). One of the main government goals for the healthcare sector in the GCC countries and specifically in the UAE is to increase the overall wellbeing of health and the healthcare industry. (UAE CABINET, 2011) MES is therefore recommended as it generates cost, time, and quality advantages which can be passed on to the payer thereby contributing to the goals of the government. Finally, MES providers also should be able to benefit by establishing gainful and sustainable businesses.

The results of the survey conducted, with regards to the medical equipment procurement and planning processes, demonstrate that there is a need for revised and standardized equipment procurement method in healthcare facilities in the UAE. This is a clear indication that there is a need for an MES that allows healthcare providers to manage and maintain equipment more efficiently and effectively. The benefits described indicate that the MES provider by virtue of having comprehensive knowledge of equipment planning and procurement, can substantially improve the quality of care. For example, equipment lifetime can be extended by providing upgrades; equipment replacement saves direct equipment ownership costs. In addition, ensuring proper user training increases the quality and efficiency of treatment and overall healthcare delivery. (David & Judd, 2000) (OEM, 2011)

The conducted survey, interviews and the secondary research have verified that non-core tasks and responsibilities of a healthcare provider (e.g. equipment management) are derailing clinicians from performing their core medical responsibilities. It is expected that demand for treatment will increase in the next few years;

solutions to reducing the burden of such responsibilities will be required.[18] In addition, due to the lack of transparency in the implementation of healthcare regulations, non-core professional responsibilities will increase if an appropriate management system is not devised (Alpen Capital Limited, 2009). High turnover rates of medical practitioners in some GCC countries and especially in UAE call for stability in both human resources and the quality of healthcare. (Zawya, 2011) Many of these non-core professional responsibilities can be passed on from the healthcare provider to the MES provider. This would enable medical practitioners to focus on the quality and efficiency of the healthcare treatment.

The cost structure of healthcare provision in the GCC and associated budgets and performance targets are not transparent in GCC (Alpen Capital Limited, 2009). While efforts are being made to increase private participation, the healthcare sector in the GCC region is still dominated by the government which is carrying the increasing cost of healthcare. The government lacks the required assistance of support services, especially in the field of technology, to create the required transparency and to reduce and stabilize costs. Support services could be used to increase transparency by reducing fluctuating indirect operational costs relating to equipment maintenance, repair and management. (Bronzino, 2000)

This could be achieved through MES. In fact governments are searching for support from international players in the private sector to increase the transparency of healthcare costs, standards and regulation. (Mourshed, Hediger, & Lambert, 2007) Governments in the GCC place high importance on raising the quality of healthcare, while private players prioritize profit maximization (HC Consultancy 1, 2011). MES is an opportunity for the government to encourage raising the quality of healthcare delivery and simultaneously allowing the private healthcare providers to increase their profit margins by achieving operational efficiency through reduced operation and administrative responsibilities. The demand in reducing the responsibilities of the government and increasing the private sector in participa-

18 65% of the respondents answered that non-core professional tasks are restricting medical practitioners from focusing on their patients needs. Secondary research for this statement refers to an analysis of information obtained; see also McKinsey and Company's *Gulf Cooperation Council Health Care: Challenges and Opportunities* report (Mourshed, Hediger, & Lambert, Gulf Cooperation Council Health Care: Challenges and Opportunities, 2007).

tion into the healthcare industry is realizable with an independent MES approach for medical equipment.

Regulations

Healthcare regulations in GCC are not at par with international standards. Through encouraging foreign private participation in the healthcare industry, especially in regards to setting standards for quality, regulations in the GCC can be strengthened (Frost & Sullivan, 2009) (Alpen Capital Limited, 2009). MES, by virtue of its long term commitment and due to the mutual interdependence of the stakeholders involved, can both raise and set the standard of healthcare upon which the healthcare regulations are based.

The MES models devised as part of this paper are recommended for implementing an MES program in the GCC region. Each of the MES Wheel service bundles identified (EES, IES, PES) can be adopted and implemented in healthcare facilities in the GCC based on their compatibility with the healthcare providers needs. The healthcare provider can thus identify the services required, and visualize the level of equipment ownership needed to achieve its long term goals though the Portfolio/ Ownership Matrix devised. Finally the Stakeholder Framework is recommended for government entities and healthcare providers to analyze the feasibility of running a theoretical MES operation. The TEI model is a recommended method for healthcare providers to analyze the costs, benefits, risks, and flexibility associated with an MES program if it were to be implemented in their facilities.

7.2 Outlook

International regulatory bodies have been recruited to assist the GCC governments in formulating regulations for the healthcare sectors in the GCC region. In order to raise the quality of healthcare in the region, international healthcare providers and operators have been recruited to mange public healthcare facilities. This is expected to increase both the quality and availability of quality of healthcare delivery in the region. (Alpen Capital Limited, 2009) According to an interview conducted with a top senior health regulatory official in UAE, the laws must be revised to enable privatisation.

Secondary research as well as the survey and the interviews conducted, have verified that general patient waiting time, especially radiology treatments/ exams such as therapeutic radiology, are very high.[19] It is expected that there will be an increase in chronic illnesses such as diabetes, heart disease, obesity, and other cardiovascular complication. Diagnosing and thereby treating these diseases all require the assistance of diagnostic radiology equipment. It is also expected that, due to the increase in the size of the aging population as well as an increase in growth of the overall population, demand for treatment will increase.

Health insurance is also expected to increase demand for healthcare and expensive treatments (e.g. radiology). Based on the Moral Hazard theory, the availability of health insurance or an increase in the coverage of health insurance tends to encourage people to opt for more expensive optional treatments that they could not have been able to afford before in the same manner that doctors are also more encouraged to recommend them. (Newhouse, 2000) This in turn could lead to demand for more complex procedures and technology leading to an overall increase in the quality of healthcare in the region. The availability of Islamic insurance (Takaful) is also expected to encourage the national population to seek treatment; the market for Takaful is expected to substantially grow by 16.1% between 2009 and 2012. (Pathak, 2010) Health insurance might therefore lead to an increase in the health expenditures per capita. (Alpen Capital Limited, 2009)

While the economy in the GCC region has suffered a blow due to financial crisis; the damage is comparatively low compared with other regions. Based on an analysis of the region's GDP, inflation rate, unemployment rate, real growth rate, and overall quality of life, level of human development, and FDI, it is expected the GCC region will continue to grow. This is especially true as investments in infrastructure have substantially increased in an effort to diversify the economy. This applies as well to the healthcare infrastructure which is being strongly promoted.

---

[19] Research is based on McKinsey & Company's *Gulf Cooperation Council Health Care: Challenges and Opportunities* as well as on Alpen Capital's report *GCC Healthcare Sector*.

The reported increase in FDI and projected growth will assist countries in the GCC region to initiate and complete planned projects (Maben, Al-Thowini, West, & Rafferty, 2009). This could positively impact the growth of the healthcare industry as more foreign private providers invest in the region. Rapid growth rate in the region also support this (Roubini Global Economics, 2011). High inflation rates however might deter the projected development.

7.3 Conclusion

The goal of this dissertation is to evaluate the success potential for an MES program in the GCC as well as to attempt establish whether it will contribute to raising the quality of healthcare delivery in GCC.

Results imply an increase in demand for basic healthcare delivery and a simultaneous increase in healthcare treatment costs. Population growth and aging populations in combination with the local health-risk factors, like cardiovascular or diabetes diseases, are factors behind the heightened demand. This demonstates the need to increase the quality of care and reduce the treatment costs to be more effective and efficient. Both the primary and secondary research indicate that there is a need for optimizing usage and maintenance of medical equipment in the GCC; this is especially true for the UAE (HC Consultancy 2, 2011) (HC Consultancy 3, 2011) (HC Consultancy 4, 2011).[20] The challenges listed represent gaps in the GCC healthcare market that can be compensated for with an MES program.

This increase in demand for healthcare services should be compensated on the one hand and on the other hand offers opportunities for quality, time and cost optimization approaches described in the Managed Equipment Services paradigm. It could be confirmed that MES is not known to the local market, however the process and approach is getting high consent under the local healthcare professionals (Frost & Sullivan, 2009) (MES Survey, 2011). The developed and discussed empirical service paradigm, the Portfolio / Ownership Matrix, the Stakeholder Framework and the Pricing method are models that demonstrate and prove a theo-

[20] Based on conducted survey, interviews and the secondary research (e.g. (Mourshed, Hediger, & Lambert, 2007).

retical MES approach into the GCC region and especially in United Arab Emirates.

Radiology devices are making an immense contribution to the health and quality of life in the GCC and especially in the UAE. However the potential of technology advancement and usage is under-utilized. Equipment upgrades and replacement have a lack of a proper equipment planning process and the critical equipment maintenance shows room for improvement in healthcare. Equipment lifetime can be increased and downtime could be decreased with MES. This again needs the capabilities of an MES provider that has the ability to run such medical equipment more efficient and effective instead of a single hospital or clinic. The connected increase in quality and reduction in costs, e.g. by less downtime and upgraded/ well maintained medical devices, could be directly passed on towards the hospital provider and the payer, matching the overall goal of the government is to increase the quality while decreasing the costs and the patient waiting time.

It has thus been concluded that MES can be a constructive addition to the GCC and especially the UAE healthcare market. However, this approach also generates risks for all involved parties by passing on the mentioned responsibilities to the MES provider. The MES provider needs to demonstrate its service to be a long-term, sustainable and trustworthy business that can actually ensure the operation of the medical equipment on the agreed level. In addition the MES provider must generate synergy effects, all while turning over a profit.

In such a case an MES provider can be an effective and efficient addition to the healthcare provider and to the healthcare system in general. As a whole, this offers the opportunity to increase the quality of care while decreasing the cost of care.

8. References

A.D.A.M. Incorporated. (2011).
Imaging and Radiology. Retrieved April 20, 2011, from National Library of Medicine: http://www.nlm.nih.gov/medlineplus/ency/article/007451.htm

Abetti, P. A., & Haldar, P. (2009, June 9).
One hundred years of superconductivity: science, technology, products, profits and industry structure. *International Journal of Technology Management, 48* (4), pp. 432-447.

Akintoye, A., & Chinyio, E. (2005).
Private Finance Initiative in the healthcare sector: trends and risk assessment. *Engineering, Construction and Architectural Management, 12* (6), pp. 601-616.

Al Mashni, R. A. (2010, March 15).
Value Partners identifies the unfulfilled potential for the Gulf Cooperation Council's insurance sector. Retrieved June 12, 2011, from http://www.ameinfo.com/226757.html

Allianz Worldwide Care. (2011, January 24).
Healthcare in Qatar. Retrieved Spetember 1, 2011, from Allianz: http://www.allianzworldwidecare.com/healthcare-in-qatar

Alpen Capital Limited. (2009).
GCC Healthcare Industry. Dubai: Alpen Capital.

Arnold, T. (2011, April 6).
GCC limits block foreign investment. Retrieved June 11, 2011, from The National: http://www.thenational.ae/business/economy/gcc-limits-block-foreign-investment

Asteral. (2011).
Asteral Sources. Retrieved September 1, 2011, from Asteral.com: http://www.asteral.com/content/resources

Asteral. (2011).
Demystifying Managed Equipment Services. Retrieved September 1, 2011, from Asteral.com: http://www.asteral.com/images/uploads/job-doc/Asteral_WP_Demystifying_MES_updated_Dec20101.pdf

Asteral. (2011).
Demystifying Managed Equipment Services. Reading: Asteral.

Asteral. (2011).
Leicester Exceeds 99% Uptime With Asteral. Retrieved June 17, 2011, from Asteral: http://www.asteral.com/news/leicester-exceeds-99-uptime-with-asteral

Asteral. (2011).
Peterborough awards first ever vendor independent radiotherapy MES in UK. Retrieved September 1, 2011, from Asteral News: http://www.asteral.com/news/peterborough-awards-first-ever-vendor-independent-radiotherapy-mes-in-uk

ATKearney. (2008).
Next generation of healthcare markets – future trends of hospital infrastructure development. Düsseldorf: ATKearney.

Ayub, M. (2003).
An Introduction to Takaful – An Alternative to Insurance. Retrieved September 1, 2011, from Islamic Economics: http://www.iefpedia.com/english/wp-content/uploads/2009/09/An-Introduction-to-Takaful-%E2%80%93-An-Alternative-to-Insurance-by-Muhammad-Ayub1.pdf

Bahrain Economic Quarterly. (2011).
Bahrain Economic Quarterly Q2 2011. Bahrain: Bahrain Economic Development Report.

Balakrishnan, S. (1999).
Quality for Life in the Medical Equipment Industry: A Case Study. *Competitiveness Review , 9* (2), pp. 36-48.

Baskan, B., & Wright, S. (2011, Spring).
SEEDS OF CHANGE: COMPARING STATE-RELIGION RELATIONS IN QATAR AND SAUDI ARABIA. *Arab Studies Quarterly , 33* (2), pp. 96-111.

Baxter, E. (2009, October 27).
Healthcare costs puts Bahrain's free service in jeopardy. Retrieved September 1, 2011, from http://www.arabianbusiness.com/property/article/571695-rising-healthcare-costs-puts-bahrains-free-service-in-jeopardy

Ben-Daya, M., Duffuaa, S. O., Raouf, A., Knezevic, J., & Ait-Kadi, D. (2009). *Handbook of Maintenance Management and Engineering.* London: Springer-Verlag.

Berger, S. (2008).
Fundamentals of Health Care Financial Management : A Practical Guide to Fiscal Issues and Activities. Hoboken, NJ, USA: Wiley.

Bitar, Z. (2009, June 16).
Dubai Contributes More than 30% of the UAE Economy. *Gulf News Online*, 3.

Blanche, E. (2001, May 1).
GCC SECURITY: NEW ALLIANCES IN THE MAKING? *Middle East* (312), p. 4.

Boughanmi, H. (2008, March).
The Trade Potential of the Arab Gulf Cooperation Countries (GCC): A Gravity Model Approach. *Journal of Economic Integration*, pp. 42-56.

Brigham, E. F., & Ehrhardt, M. C. (2009).
Financial Management Theory and Practice (13 ed.). Mason: South-Western Cengage Learning.

Brigham, E. F., & Houston, J. F. (2009).
Fundamentals of Financial Management (Book Only) (12th Edition ed.). Mason: South-Western, Cengage Learning.

Bronzino, J. D. (2000).
The biomedical engineering handbook (Vol. 2). Florida: CRC Press, LLC.

Bu-Alayyan, S., Mostafa, A., Al-Etaibi, B., Sorkhou, E., Al-Taher, H., & Al-Weqayyan, A. (2008).
Patient Satisfaction with Primary Health Care Services in Kuwait. *Kuwait Medical Journal*, 25-30.

Business Monitor International. (2009, Q3).
United Arab Emirates Q3 2009. UAE.

Business Monitor International. (2009, Q4).
Saudi Arabia Q4 2009. KSA.

Business Monitor International. (2010, January 18).
Kuwait Pharmaceuticals and Healthcare Report Q1 2010. Kuwait City, Kuwait.

Cameron, J. (2003).
Managing medical equipment in public hospitals. Melbourne: Auditor General Victoria.

Central Statistical Department. (2007).
Statistics for 2007. Dubai: MOH - Ministry of Health.

Central Statistical Department. (2009).
Statistics for 2009. Dubai: MOH - Ministry of Health.

Chan, A. Y. (2003).
Medical Technology Management Practice. Illinois: Charles C Thomas, Ltd.

Chandriani, D. G. (2010, April 05).
Biomedical Devices- Planning & Procurement Considerations. Retrieved June 11, 2011, from Technecon Healthcare:
http://techneconhealthcare.com/article_details.php?id=17

Chawla, M. (2007).
Healthcare Spending in the New EU Memeber States. *World Bank Working Papers*, 23.

Chemingui, M. A. (2008, May 1).
Petroleum revenues in Gulf Cooperation Council, countries and their labor market paradox. *Journal of Policy Modeling, 30* (3), pp. 491-503.

CIA. (2011, August 23).
Central Intelligence Agency. Retrieved August 31, 2011, from The World Fact Book: https://www.cia.gov/library/publications/the-world-factbook/

Collins English Dictionary - Complete & Unabridged 10th Edition. (n.d.).
Equipment. Retrieved September 1, 2011, from Dictionary.com:
http://dictionary.reference.com/cite.html?qh=equipment&ia=ced

Collins English Dictionary - Complete & Unabridged 10th Edition. (n.d.).
Service. Retrieved September 1, 2011, from Dictionary.com:
http://dictionary.reference.com/browse/service

Collins English Dictionary. (2011, January 15).
Equipment. Retrieved September 1, 2011, from Dictionary.com:
http://dictionary.reference.com/browse/Equipment

Conbeer, G. P. (2007, June).
Making the Right Long-term Prescription for Medical Equipment Financing. *The CBS Interactive Business Network. Healthcare Financial Management*, 1.

Contino, R. M. (2006).
The Complete Equipment-Leasing Handbook: A Deal Maker's Guide with Forms, Checklists, and Worksheets. New York: AMACOM/American Management Association.

Costales, S. B., & Szurovy, G. (1994).
The guide to understanding financial statements (2nd Edition ed.). Mason: McGraw Hill, Inc.

Cowan, J. (2000).
Clinical Risk - Minimising Harm in Practical Procedures and Use of Equipment. *Clinical Governance, 5* (4), 245-249.

Dain, S. (2002).
Normal Accidents: Human Error and Medical Equipment Design. *The Heart Surgery Forum*, 254-257.

Daman. (2011, January 10).
Thiqa Program. Retrieved June 24, 2011, from Daman Health: http://www.damanhealth.ae/eDaman/en/AboutDaman/CorporateProfile/thiqaProgram.html?div=corporateProfile&subdiv=submenu6

David, Y., & Judd, T. M. (2000).
Management and Assessment of Medical Technology. In J. D. Bronzino, *The biomedical engineering handbook* (Second Edition, Vol. II, pp. 168-8 - 168-13). Heidelberg: Springer.

Davidson, L. A. (1986, August).
Central Service as a Clinical Department. *Hospital Materiel Management Quarterly, 8* (1), p. 91.

DHCC Press Coverage. (2011).
Dubai Health City Press Coverage. Dubai, United Arab Emirates.

DHCC. (2011, June 11).
The Center for Healthcare Planning and Quality. Retrieved June 12, 2011, from Dubai Healthcare City: http://www.dhcc.ae/standards/

DHCC. (2011).
The home of world-class healthcare. Retrieved June 2, 2011, from Dubai Healthcare City: http://www.dhcc.ae/about-us/

Dictionary.com Unabridged. (n.d.).
service. Retrieved September 1, 2011, from Dictionary.com: http://dictionary.reference.com/browse/service

Diener, E., & Suh, E. (1997, June 2).
Measuring Quality of Life: Economic, Social and subjective indicators. *Social Indicators Research*, pp. 189-216.

Division, Federal Research. (2007, July 2).
Country profile: United Arab Emirates (UAE). *Country Profile: United Arab Emirates*. Abu Dhabi, UAE: Library of Congress.

Dolan, A. M. (2004).
Risk Management of Medical Devices: Ensuring Safety and Efficacy through ISO 14971. *ASQ World Conference on Quality and Improvement Proceedings, 58*, pp. 69-72.

Duggirala, M., Rajendran, C., & Anantharaman, R. N. (2008).
Provider-Perceived Dimensions of Total Quality Management in Healthcare. *Benchmarking: An International Journal, 15* (6), pp. 693-722.

Dunham-Taylor, J., & Pinczuk, J. Z. (2010).
Financial Management for Nurse Managers: Merging the Heart with the Dollar (2 ed.). Sudbury: Jones and Bartlett.

Dyro, J. F. (2004).
Clinical Engineering Handbook. New York: Academic Press.

E Lakhan, S., Kaplan, A., Laird, C., & Leiter, Y. (2009, September 9).
The Interventionalism of Medicine: Interventiona Rradiology, Cardiology, and Neuroradiology. *International Archives of Medicine*, 1-27 & 2-27.

Egbert, C. (2009, September 22).
Top 10 healthcare projects in the GCC. Abu Dhabi.

El-Haik, B., & Mekki, K. S. (2008).
Medical Device Design for Six Sigma: A Road Map for Safety and Effectiveness. Hoboken, New Jersy, USA: Wiley.

EMRO, R. H. (2011).
Information of: OMAN. Retrieved September 1, 2011, from http://gis.emro.who.int/HealthSystemObservatory/PDF/Oman/Health%20system%20organization.pdf

Encyclopædia Britannica. (2011, January 15).
Encyclopædia Britannica Online. Retrieved August 31, 2011, from Encyclopædia Britannica: http://www.britannica.com/

Encyclopædia Britannica. (2011).
Health Care. Retrieved September 1, 2011, from Encyclopædia Britannica Online: http://www.britannica.com/EBchecked/topic/258213/health-care

Encyclopædia Britannica. (2011).
original-equipment manufacturer. Retrieved September 1, 2011, from Encyclopædia Britannica Online: http://www.britannica.com/EBchecked/topic/432557/original-equipment-manufacturer

Encyclopædia Britannica. (2011).
Original Equipment Manufacturer. Retrieved September 1, 2011, from Encyclopædia Britannica Online:
http://www.britannica.com/EBchecked/topic/432557/original-equipment-manufacturer

Englard, B. (2007).
Schaum's Outline of Intermediate Accounting II (2 ed.). Ohio: McGraw Hill.

Espicom Business Intelligence. (2009).
Saudi Arabia Medistat Outlook QII 2009. UK: British Library Cataloguing in Publication Data.

Espicom Business Intelligence. (2010).
The World Medical Markets Fact Book 2010. UK: British Library Cataloguing in Publication Data.

Forrester Research Inc. (2009).
The Total Economic Impact Of Microsoft Exchange 2010. New York: Forrester Research, Inc.

Frost, & Sullivan. (2009).
The GCC Healthcare Industry Outlook. Abu Dhabi: Frost and Sullivan.

Gapenski, L. C. (2004).
Healthcare finance: an introduction to accounting and financial management. Arlington: AUPHA/HAP.

Garman, T., & Forgue, R. (2009).
Personal Finance (10th Edition ed.). Mason: South-Western Cengage Learning.

GE Healthcare. (2010, November 1).
Hospital and Healthcare Solutions. Retrieved September 1, 2011, from GE Healthcare Product Technology - Managed Equipment Service:
http://www.gehealthcare.com/euen/hospital_solutions/managed-equipment-service.html

General Electric. (2011, March 2).
Stock Information. Retrieved September 1, 2011, from GE Imagination at Work:
http://www.ge.com/investors/stock_info/index.html

General Electric Company. (2011).
Hospital and Healthcare Solutions. Retrieved September 1, 2011, from GE Healthcare : http://www.gehealthcare.com/euen/hospital_solutions/managed-equipment-service.html

Global Health Expenditure Database. (2009).
NHA Indicators. Retrieved August 31, 2011, from http://apps.who.int/nha/database/ChoiceDataExplorerRegime.aspx

Global Health Observatory. (2011, January 9).
Wolrd Health Organization: Data and statistics. Retrieved August 31, 2011, from http://www.who.int/research/en/

Global Security. (2011).
Gulf Cooperation Council [GCC]. Retrieved August 31, 2011, from http://www.globalsecurity.org/military/world/gulf/gcc.htm

Government Health, E. (2011, August 4).
Government Health Executive Interview. (M. J. Kloep, Interviewer)

Government of Dubai. (2010, June 19).
Strategic Goals. Retrieved May 18, 2011, from Dubai Health Authority: http://www.dohms.gov.ae/En/aboutus/pages/strategicgoals.aspx

Griffin, D. J. (2010).
Hospitals What They Are and How They Work (4 ed.). Sundbury, Massachusetts: Jones & Bartlett Learning.

Gruen, R., & Howarth, A. (2005).
Financial Management in Health Services. Maidenhead, GBR: McGraw-Hill Education.

Gulácsi, L., Dávid, T., & Dózsa, C. (2002, December). Pricing and reimbursement of drugs and medical devices in Hungary.
The European Journal of Health Economics : HEPAC , 3 (4), pp. 271-278.

HAAD. (2009, June 10).
Health Statistics 2009. Retrieved September 1, 2011, from Health Authority - Abu Dhabi: http://www.haad.ae/haad/tabid/37/Default.aspx?Search=statistics

Haarlander, S., Buhner, A., Schwandt, M., & Schoffski, O. (2007).
Public Private Partnership (PPP) im Krankenhausbereich. Burgdorf: HERZ.

Hamdy, H., Telmesani, A. W., Wardy, N., Abdel-Khalek, N., Carruthers, G., Hassan, F., et al. (2010, April).
Undergraduate medical education in the Gulf Cooperation Council: A multi-countries study, Part 1 & 2. *Medical Teacher, 32* (4), pp. 290-295.

Hanna, K. E. (2001).
Innovation and Invention in Medical Devices: Workshop Summary. Washington,

DC, USA: National Academies Press.

Harb, N. (2009, November 8).
Oil Exports, Non-Oil GDP, and Investment in the GCC Countries. *Review of Development Economics*, pp. 695-708.

Hardy, P. A. (2004, May/June).
Getting a Return on Investment from Spending Capital Dollars on New Beds. *Journal of Healthcare Management, 49* (3), pp. 199-205.

Hashem, A. (2007).
Cooperation Council for the Arab States of the Gulf *(GCC).* Carlisle, PA: U.S. Army War College.

HC Consultancy 1, CEO. (2011, July 18).
Regional GCC Healthcare Consultancy Interview with CEO. (M. J. Kloep, Interviewer)

HC Consultancy 2, Partner. (2011, June 21).
International Healthcare Consultancy 2 with Partner. *International Healthcare Consultancy 2 Interview*. (M. J. Kloep, Interviewer)

HC Consultancy 3, Director. (2011, June 22).
International Healthcare Consultancy 3 Interview with Director. (M. J. Kloep, Interviewer)

HC Consultancy 4, Manager. (2011, August 11).
International Healthcare Consultancy 4 Interview with Manger. (M. J. Kloep, Interviewer)

Health Authority. (2011).
About HAAD. Retrieved May 18, 2011, from Health Authority - Abu Dhabi: http://www.haad.ae/haad/tabid/59/Default.aspx

Healthcare Provider 1, COO. (2011, March 25).
Personal Communication. (M. J. Kloep, Interviewer)

Healthcare Provider 2, Radiologist. (2011, April 5).
Personal Communication. (M. J. Kloep, Interviewer)

Helem, C. M. (2011).
Persian Gulf States: A Country Study. Retrieved September 31, 2011, from Library of Congress: http://countrystudies.us/persian-gulf-states/

Holdford, D. A., & Brown, T. R. (2010).
Introduction to Hospital and Health-System Pharmacy Practice. Wisconsin:

American Society of Health-System Pharmacists (ASHP).

Huges, R. (2003).
Living & Working in the Gulf States & Saudi Arabia: A Survival Handbook. London: Survival Print.

Huizenga, E. (2004).
Innovation management in the ICT sector: how frontrunners stay ahead. Cheltenham: Edward Elgar Publishing Limited.

Hungenberg, H. (2003).
Fokussierung versus Diversifikation - Überlegungen zur Zukunft der "Multibusiness Firm". Erlangen-Nürnberg: Institut für Unternehmungsplanung.

Hungenberg, H., & Wulf, T. (2004).
Grundlagen der Unternehmensführung (3. Auflage). Berlin, Heidelberg, New York: Springer-Verlag.

Hungenberg, H., & Wulf, T. (2005).
Strategisches Management – Was die Wissenschaft für die Praxis leisten kann. In H. M. Hungenberg, *Handbuch strategisches Management* (2nd Edition, pp. 207-208). Wiesbaden: Gabler.

Imoh, A., & Mutshinda, C. M. (2010, April 1).
Health status assessment using reverse supply chain data: MRN. *Management Research Review, 33* (2), pp. 111-122.

International Living. (2010, February 10).
2010 Quality of Life Index: 194 Countries Ranked and Rated to Reveal the Best Places to Live. (Publishing, Ltd.) Retrieved August 31, 2011, from International Living: http://internationalliving.com/2010/02/quality-of-life-2010/#

Jacobus, C. J. (2008).
Texas Real Estate (10 ed.). Mason: Thomson South-Western.

Jin-Li, H., & Yuan-Fu, H. (2004, December).
Technical Efficiencies in Large Hospitals: A Managerial Perspective. *International Journal of Management, 21* (4), pp. 506-513.

Johns Hopkins Medicine International. (2010, December 15).
Tawam Molecular Imaging Centre - Al Ain, Abu Dhabi, United Arab Emirates. Retrieved June 2011, 2011, from John Hopkins Medicine: http://www.hopkinsmedicine.org/international/international_affiliations/clinical_operation/tawam_molecular_imaging_centre.html

Journal of Vascular Interventional Radiology. (2010).
Global Statement Defining Interventional Radiology. *Journal of Vascular Interventional Radiology , 21* (8), 1147-1149.

Judd, T. M. (2004).
Health Technology Management (Section 3). In J. F. Dyro, *Clinical Engineering Handbook* (pp. 99-102, 34-38,). Amsterdam: Academic Press.

K. Aaronson, N., Ahmedzai, S., Bergman, B., Bullinger, M., Cull, A., J. Duez, N., et al. (1992, November 30).
The European Organization for Research and Treatment of Cancer QLQ-C30: A Quality-of-Life Instrument for use in International Clinical Trials in Oncology. *Journal of the National Cancer Institute*, pp. 365-376.

Kapil, S. (2011).
Financial Management. Mumbai: Pearson - Dorling Kindersley.

Karoly, L. (2010, September 24).
The Role of Education in Preparing Graduates for the Labor Market in the GCC Countries. *RAND Corporation Publications Department*, pp. 50-54.

Keller, J. P. (2004).
Compartive Evaluation of Medical Devices. In J. F. Dyro, *Clinical Engineering Handbook* (pp. 367-369). Amsterdam: Elsavier Academic Press.

Kensett, R. G. (1990).
Changing Scene of Health Care and Technology. *Proceedings of the 11th Congress of the International Federation of Hospital Engineering* (p. 88-91). London: Chapman & Hall.

Khan, M. S. (2009, April 1).
The GCC Monetary Union: Choice of Exchange Rate Regime. *Working Paper Series*, pp. 1-13.

Kimber, R. J., Jones, R., & Cornwell, C. D. (1983, March).
To Rent . . . Or Not to Rentome Financial Concepts of Rentingental Tips of the Trade. *Quality, 22* (3), p. 27.

Kinninmont, J. (2009).
The GCC in 2020: Outlook for the Gulf and the Global Economy. Doha, Qatar: Economist Intelligence Unit.

Klass, D., & Goss, R. (2003, November 2).
The Politics of grief and continuing bonds with the dead: the cases of maoist China and Wahhabi Islam. *Death Studies, 27* (9), p. 787.

Klugman, J. (2010).
The Real Wealth of Nations: Pathways to Human Development. Human Development Report 2010. New York: Palgrave Macmillan.

Lane, S. G., Longstreth, E., & Nixon, V. (2001).
A community leader's guide to hospital finance: evaluating how a hospital gets and spends its money. Boston: Project Access.

Lavy, S., & Shohet, I. (2009).
Integrated healthcare facilities maintenance management model: case studies. *Facilities, 27* (3/4), pp. 107-119.

Lincoln, J. E. (2009, Autumn).
Product Risk Management Under ISO 14971:2007. *Journal of Validation Technology, 15* (4), pp. 10-18.

Lindgreen, A., Antioco, M., & Harness, D. (2009, April).
Purchasing and Marketing of Social and Environmental Sustainability for High-Tech Medical Equipment. *Journal of Business Ethics, suppl. Supplement, 85*, pp. 445-462.

Lindgreen, A., Antioco, M., & Harness, D. (2009, April).
Purchasing and Marketing of Social and Environmental Sustainability for High-Tech Medical Equipment. *Journal of Business Ethics, 85*, pp. 445-462.

Litteral, L. A., & Altay, N. (2011).
Service Parts Management: Demand Forecasting and Inventory Control. London: Springer-Verlag.

Liu, H., Yang, H., Yang, J., & Dai, R. (2008).
Study on a Model of the Equipment MRO Service Information Systems. *Management Science and Engineering, 2* (2), 43-48.

Longenecker, J. G., Moore, C. W., Palich, L. E., & Petty, J. W. (2006).
Small business management: an entrepreneurial emphasis. Mason: South-Western.

Loper, D. L. (1993).
Issues of Materiel Management in the Neonatal Intensive Care. *Hospital Material Management Quarterly, 15* (2), 13.

Lopiano, M., & Del Fava, R. (2008).
Medical imaging. Retrieved May 29, 2011, from Access Science: http://accessscience.com/content/Medical%20imaging/412850

Lusted, L. B. (2008).
Radiology. Retrieved May 29, 2011, from Access Science: http://accessscience.com/content/Radiology/570700

Maben, J., Al-Thowini, K., West, E., & Rafferty, A.-M. (2009, July 21).
Uneven Development: Comparing the indigenous healthcare workforce in Saudi Arabia, Bahrain and Oman. *International Journal of Nursing Studies*, pp. 392-396.

MadeGowda, J. (2007).
Management Accounting (1st Edition ed.). Mumbai: Himalaya Pub. House.

Maine. (2003, Fall).
Maine's adaptive equipment loan program: Creative financing for assistive technology. *Journal of Disability Policy Studies, 14* (2), pp. 82-85.

Maisel, S., & Shoup, J. A. (2009).
Saudi Arabia and the Gulf Arab States Today: A-J. Westport, CT: Greenwood Press.

Marcinko, D. E. (2006).
Dictionary of Health Insurance and Managed Care. New York: Springer Publishing Company, Inc.

McGillivray, M. (1991, October 10).
The human development index: Yet another redundant composite development indicator? *World Development, 19* (10), pp. 1461-1468.

McGinley, S. (2010, June 29).
Health chief sees mandatory insurance in Dubai soon. Retrieved September 1, 2011, from http://www.arabianbusiness.com/health-chief-sees-mandatory-insurance-in-dubai-soon-293632.html

MES Provider 1, CEO (2010, June 20).
MES Provider 1 Interview with CEO & Founder. (M. J. Kloep, Interviewer)

MES Provider 2, Director. (2010, June 24).
MES Provider 2 Interview with Director. (M. J. Kloep, Interviewer)

MES Survey. (2011, August).
Personal Communication.

Millennium Research Group. (2011, January 9).
Tough Times Ahead for OEM Diagnostic Imaging Equipment Service Providers, GE and Siemens. Retrieved September 1, 2011, from PR Newswire:

http://www.prnewswire.com/news-releases/tough-times-ahead-for-oem-diagnostic-imaging-equipment-service-providers-ge-and-siemens-99224844.html

Miltenburg, J. (2005).
Manufacturing strategy: how to formulate and implement a winning plan (2nd Edition ed.). New York: Productivity Press.

Mina, W. (2007, July 6).
Are the GCC FDI Location Determinants Favorable? *Economics Discussion Papers*, pp. 1-30.

Mishra, R. (2006).
Reliability and Maintenance Engineering. New Delhi: New Age International Publishers.

Montana, P. J., & Charnov, B. H. (2000).
Management (3 ed.). New York: Barron's Educational Series Incorporated.

Montana, P. J., & Charnov, B. H. (2008).
Management (4th Edition ed.). New York: Barron's Educational Series, Inc.

Morris, M. (2009, October 14).
GCC oil/gas reserves valued at $18.3tn. Retrieved August 31, 2011, from http://www.arabianbusiness.com/gcc-oil-gas-reserves-valued-at-18-3tn-11814.html

Morsy, H., & Kandil, M. E. (2009).
Determinants of Inflation in GCC. *IMF Working Papers, 9* (82), 32.

Mourshed, M., Hediger, V., & Lambert, T. (2007).
Gulf Cooperation Council Health Care: Challenges and Opportunities. p. 64.

Mourshed, M., Hediger, V., & Lambert, T. (2007, March 01.03.2007).
Private solutions for health care in the Gulf. pp. 51- 60.

Mowery, D. C., Oxley, J. E., & Silverman, B. S. (1996, July 15).
Strategic Alliances and Interfirm Knowledge Transfer. *Strategic Management Journal, 17*, pp. 77-91.

Moyer, R. C., McGuigan, J. R., & Kretlow, W. J. (2009).
Contemporary Financial Management (7 ed.). Mason: South-Western Cengage Learning.

Mubadala. (2010, June 20).
Mubadala Infrastructure. Retrieved August 31, 2011, from http://www.mubadala.ae/sectors/infrastructure

Muellner, A., Glazer, G. M., Reiser, M. F., Bradley Jr., W. G., Krestin, G. P., Hricak, H., et al. (2009).
Advancing Radiology Through Informed Leadership: Summary of the Proceedings of the Seventh Biannual Symposium of the International Society for Strategic Studies in Radiology (IS3R), 23–25 August 2007. *European Radiology Journal, 19* (8), 1-2.

Mufti, M. H. (2002).
Healthcare development strategies in the Kingdom of Saudi Arabia. New York: Kluwer Academic Publishers.

Nah, S.-H., & Osifo-Dawodu, E. (2007).
Establishing private health care facilities in developing countries: a guide for medical entrepreneurs. World Bank Institute.

Nah, S.-H., & Osifo-Dawodu, E. (2007).
WBI Development Studies: Establishing Private Health Care Facilities in Developing Countries: A Guide for Medical Entrepreneursrs. Herndon: World Bank Publications.

National Institute for Foreign Trade. (2011).
UAE Market report Medical Equipment. Dubai: Italian Trade Comission.

NCB. (2011).
NCB: Saudi Healthcare Sector Report - 2011. Abu Dhabi: Zawya.

Nevitt, P. K., & Fabozzi, F. J. (2000).
Project Financing (7th Edition ed.). London: Euromoney Books.

Newhouse, J. (2000).
Handbook of health economics (1st Edition ed., Vol. 1). Amsterdam: Elsevier Science B.V.

News Medical: Research and Market. (2010, May 11).
Bahrain pharmaceutical market to grow to $120mn in 2010. Retrieved September 1, 2011, from http://www.news-medical.net/news/20100511/Bahrain-pharmaceutical-market-to-grow-to-24120mn-in-2010.aspx

Nichols, H. L., & Day, D. A. (2010).
Moving the earth: the workbook of excavation (6th Edition ed.). New York: McGraw Hill Professional.

OEM MES Provider, Project Leader (2011, July 20).
OEM MES Provider Interview with MES Project Leader. (M. J. Kloep, Interviewer)

OEM, Service Manager (2011, June 20).
OEM Interview with Service Manager. (M. J. Kloep, Interviewer)

Office of the Chief Economist. (2010, April).
Inflation in Saudi Arabia: Drivers, Trends, and Outlook. Retrieved August 31, 2011, from Samba Financial Group:
http://www.samba.com.sa/GblDocs/Inflation_in_Saudi_Arabia_Eng.pdf

O'Grady, J., & Griffin, J. P. (2003).
The Regulation of Medical Products. Australia: BMJ Books.

Osborn, R. C. (1965).
Business Finance The Management Approach. New York: Appleton-Century-Crofts, Meredith Publishing Company.

Parmenter, D. (2010).
Key Performance Indicators: Developing, Implementing, and Using Winning KPIs (2nd Edition). New Jersey: John Wiley & Sons, Inc.

Pathak, S. (2010, January 14).
Takaful market to grow faster than conventional insurance. Retrieved September 1, 2011, from
http://www.zawya.com/story.cfm/sidZAWYA20100114044449/?relcontent=ZAWYA20080303071710

Pathak, Shveta. (2010, May 19).
GCC to hold 70.4% share in Takaful growth. Retrieved September 1, 2011, from
http://www.emiratesfn.com/news/newsfull.php?newid=371640

Pathology in Practice. (2007, August).
A closer look at Managed Equipment Services. Retrieved September 1, 2011, from Pathology in Practice:
http://www.pathologyinpractice.com/Story.aspx?Story=417

Pehlchen, B. (2003).
Leasing - "It is the Use of Equipment, Not the Ownership, that Generates Profit". Auflage: GRIN Verlag.

Pentagon Healthcare. (2008).
Case Study: Managed Equipment Services: Equipment Review. Retrieved June 5, 2011, from Pentagon Healthcare - Home:
http://www.pentagonhealthcare.com/case-studies.htm

Peter R. Hoskins, K. M. (2010).
Diagnostic Ultrasound: Physics and Equipment By. Campridge: Cambridge

University Press.

Philips. (2010).
Annual document for Koninklijke Philips Electronics N.V. Amsterdam: Philips.

Philips. (2011).
Case Studies - The benefits of Enterprise-wide PACS . Retrieved April 24, 2011, from Philips.com:
http://www.healthcare.philips.com/main/products/healthcare_informatics/products/enterprise_imaging_informatics/isite_pacs/testimonials/case_studies.wpd

Pooler, V. H., Pooler, D. J., & Farney, S. D. (2004).
Global purchasing and supply management: fulfill the vision (2 ed.). New York, Boston, Dordrecht, London, Moscow: Kluwer Academic Publishers.

Population Division, DESA. (2011).
World Population Ageing 1950-2050. Retrieved August 31, 2011, from Department of Economic and Social Affairs:
http://www.un.org/esa/population/publications/worldageing19502050/pdf/204unite.pdf

Porter, M. E. (2008).
The five competitive forces that shape strategy. Harvard: Harvard Business School Publishing.

Power, M. J., Desouza, K. C., & Bonifazi, C. (2006).
The Outsourcing Handbook: How to Implement a Successful Outsourcing Process. London: Kogan Page Limited.

Pratt, D. J. (2011).
Fundamentals of Construction Estimating (3 ed.). New York: Delmar Cengage Learning.

Rahman, S. (2009, December 6).
Gulf health care industry set to reach $55b by 2020. Dubai.

Regional Committee for the Eastern Mediterranean. (2006).
Technical discussions. *Fifty-Third Session* (pp. 1-17). World Health Organization.

Rehman, A. A. (2008).
Dubai & Co: global strategies for doing business in the Gulf states. Ohio: McGraw Hill, Inc.

Rodríguez, H., & Aguirre, B. E. (2006, Fall).
Hurricane Katrina and the Healthcare Infrastructure: A Focus on Disaster

Preparedness, Response, and Resiliency. *Frontiers of Health Services Management, 23* (1), pp. 12-23.

Roubini Global Economics. (2011).
Qatar: Monetary Stance and Price Dynamics (Inflation/Deflation). New York: Roubini Global Economics, LLC.

Roubini Global Economics. (2011).
United Arab Emirates: Monetary Stance and Price Dynamics (Inflation/Deflation). New York: Roubini Global Economics, LLC.

Rourke, B. M. (2008).
The Gulf Cooperation Council as a Regional Partner in Deterrence. Joint Military Operations. Newport, R.I.: Naval War College.

Saberi, M. (2010, July 14).
Residents spend Dh7.2b on treatment abroad: report. Retrieved April 18, 2011, from Gulf News: http://gulfnews.com/news/gulf/uae/health/residents-spend-dh7-2b-on-treatment-abroad-report-1.653968

Sacher, S., & Louis, S. (1998, July).
Antitrust issues in defining the product market for hospital services. *International Journal of the Economics of Business, 5* (2), pp. 181-202.

Salameh, K., Rahman, S., Al-Rifai, H., Masoud, A., Lutfi, S., Abdouh, G., et al. (2009).
An analytic study of the trends in perinatal and neonatal mortality rates in the State of Qatar over a 30-year period (1977 to 2007): a comparative study with regional and developed countries. *Journal of Perinatology*, 1.

Sallas, B., Lane, S., Mathews, R., Watkins, T., & Wiley-Patton, S. (2007, Winter).
An iterative assessment approach to improve technology adoption and implementation decisions by healthcare managers. *Information Systems Management , 24* (1), pp. 43-57.

Sambidge, A. (2010, January 12).
High growth predicted for GCC healthcare sector. Dubai.

SCAD. (2011, January 15).
GDP Share. Retrieved June 2, 2011, from Statistics Center Abu Dhabi: http://www.scad.ae/en/Statistics/Pages/SubTopicDetails.aspx?SubTopicID=102&TabID=1

Schmitt-Rüth, S., Esslinger, A. S., & Schöffski, O. (2007).
Geschichte der Medizintechnik – Markt für Medizintechnik – Zukunft des Marktes

für Medizintechnik (Erste Auflage Ausg.). Burgdorf: Herz.

Schöffski, O., & Schulenburg, J.-M. G. (2008). *Gesundheitsökonomische Evaluationen* (dritte, vollständig überarbeitete Auflage ed.). Berlin, Heidelberg, New York: Springer.

SEHA. (2009). *SEHA Formation*. Retrieved May 18, 2011, from Abu Dhabi Health Services Co.: http://www.seha.ae/seha/en/Pages/SehaFormation.aspx

Shah, M., Dayeh, I., Blatherwick, H., & Sakaedani, H. (2007). The Ḥanbalī School of Law and Ibn Taymiyya: Conflict or Conciliation. *Journal of Qur'anic Studies, 9* (2), pp. 88-114.

Shediac, R., Hashemi, A., & Bhatia, K. (2009). *The GCC's Insurance Mandate How a Healthcare Policy Shift Affects Stakeholders.* Abu Dhabi: Booz & Co.

Shi, L., & Singh, D. A. (2008). *Delivering health care in America: a systems approach* (4th Edition ed.). Ontario: Jone and Bartlett Publishing.

Shim, J. K., & Siegel, J. G. (2009). *Schaum's Outline of Financial Management* (3 ed.). Ohio: McGraw Hill Professional.

Siemens AG. (2007, April). *Bartnet Hospital*. Retrieved April 2011, 2011, from Medical.Siemens.com: medical.siemens.com

Siemens AG. (2004, July). *Case Study: Queens Hospital*. Retrieved April 24, 2011, from Medical.Siemens.com: medical.siemens.com

Siemens AG. (2011). *Understanding Managed Equipment Services (MES)*. Retrieved April 20, 2011, from Siemens Healthcare: http://www.medical.siemens.com/webapp/wcs/stores/servlet/CategoryDisplay~q_catalogId~e_-18~a_categoryId~e_1035067~a_catTree~e_100003,1035067~a_langId~e_-18~a_storeId~e_10001.htm

Sihler, W. W., Crawford, R., & Davis, H. A. (2004). *Smart Financial Management: the Essential Reference for the Successful Small Business.* New York: Amacom.

Singh, D. A., & Shi, L. (2008). *Delivering health care in America: A Systems approach* (4 ed.). Sudbury: Jones & Bartlett Learning.

Smith, A. D., & Correa, J. (2005). Value-added benefits of technology: E-procurement and e-commerce related to the health care industry. *International Journal of Health Care Quality Assurance, 18* (6/7), pp. 458-473.

Smith, P. A. (2009, October). Will the GCC finally dump the Dollar? *Middle East* (404), pp. 55-59.

Staff Report Mubadala. (2007, February 7). *Mubadala signs deal with Siemens unit*. Retrieved September 1, 2011, from Gulf News Online: http://gulfnews.com/business/general/mubadala-signs-deal-with-siemens-unit-1.160218

Statistics Centre - Abu Dhabi. (2011, June 10). *Industry and Business*. Retrieved June 2, 2011, from SCAD - Theme Tree: http://www.scad.ae/en/Statistics/Pages/ThemeTree.aspx?ThemeID=3

Stevens, R. E., Mansfield, P., Loudon, D. L., Wrenn, B., & Warren, W. E. (2006). *Marketing Planning Guide* (3rd Edition ed.). New York: Haworth.

Subba Rao, P. (2010). *Strategic Management.* Mumbai: Himalaya Pub. House.

Swamidass, P. M. (2000). *Encyclopedia of production and manufacturing management.* Massachusetts: Kluwer Academic Publishers.

Taghipour, S., Banjevic, D., & Jardine, A. K. (2011, September). Prioritization of medical equipment for maintenance decisions. *The Journal of the Operational Research Society, 62* (9), pp. 1666-1687.

Tatchell, J. (2009). *A diamond in the desert: behind the scenes in the world's richest city.* London: Sceptre.

Tavakoli, H., Karami, M., Rezai, J., Esfandiari, K., & Khashayar, P. (2007). When renewing medical equipment is necessary: a case report. *International Journal of Health Care Quality Assurance, 20* (7), pp. 616-619.

Taylor, J. (2006). *The Future of Equipment Leasing* (1 ed.). Business and Economics.

The Free Library. (2009, October 15). *GCC foreign direct investment inflows up 32pc.* Retrieved August 31, 2011, from http://www.thefreelibrary.com/GCC+foreign+direct+investment+inflows+up+32pc.-a0209781866

The Middle East. (2011, March 14). *Economic Update Kuwait*. Retrieved August 31, 2011, from Health in focus: http://www.oxfordbusinessgroup.com/economic_updates/kuwait-health-focus

Thompson, R. (2009). Gulf is rising to the healthcare challenge. *MEED: Middle East Economic Digest*, 1.

U.S. Food and Drug Administration. (2011). *Radiography*. Retrieved April 21, 2011, from FDA: http://www.fda.gov/Radiation-EmittingProducts/RadiationEmittingProductsandProcedures/MedicalImaging/MedicalX-Rays/ucm175028.htm

U.S.-Saudi Arabian Business Council. (2010, September 9). *Saudi Arabia Releases 2010 Budget*. Retrieved August 20, 2011, from http://www.us-sabc.org/custom/news/details.cfm?id=559

U.S.-U.A.E. Business Council. (2011, Feburary 8). *Commercial Trade & Foreign Direct Investment*. Retrieved June 11, 2011, from U.S.-U.A.E. Business Council: http://www.usuaebusiness.org/index.cfm?fuseaction=section.home&id=71

UAE CABINET. (2011). *UAE Government Strategy 2011 - 2013*. Retrieved September 1, 2011, from UAE Government Strategy: http://www.uaecabinet.ae/English/Documents/PMO%20StrategyDocEngFinV2.pdf

Van Horne, J. C., & Wachowicz, J. M. (2005). *Fundamentals of financial management* (13 ed.). Ohio: Financial Times Prentice Hall.

WAM. (2011, May 14). *Ministry of Health Begins Health Accreditation Implementation Plan*. Retrieved May 18, 2011, from Zawya.com: http://www.zawya.com/marketing.cfm?zp&p=/story.cfm/sidWAM20110514104031421/UAE_Ministry_of_Health_Begins_Health_Accreditation_Implementation_Plan

Weaver, S. C., & Weston, J. F. (2008). *Strategic financial management: applications of corporate finance*. Mason: Thomson South-Western.

Weishaupt, D., Köchli, V. D., & Marinček, B. (2006). *How does MRI work?: An introduction to the physics and function of magnetic resonance imaging* (2nd ed.). Berlin: Springer.

Weltman, B., & Raeburn, V. (2007). *The Rational Guide to Building Small Business Credit*. Rollinsford: Rational Press.

Wheelen, T. L., & Hunger, D. (2009). *Strategic Management and Business Policy: Achieving Sustainability* (12th ed.). New Jersey: Prentice Hall.

Whittington Health. (2011). *The Whittington Hospital NHS Trust*. Retrieved April 24, 2011, from Whittington NHS: http://www.whittington.nhs.uk/

WHO. (2010). *WHO Statistical Information System (WHOSIS)*. Retrieved September 1, 2011, from World Health Organization:

http://www.who.int/whosis/whostat/EN_WHS10_Full.pdf

WHO, U. N. (2008). *Transnational Corporations, and the Infrastructure Challenge.* New York and Geneva: United Nations.

WHO, World Health Organization. (2010). *Medical devices: managing the mismatch: an outcome of the priority medical devices project.* Geneva: WHO Press.

WHOSIS. (2010). *World Health Statistics 2010.* World Health Organization (WHO), WHO Statistical Information System.

Wolper, L. F. (2004). *Health care administration: planning, implementing, and managing organized delivery systems* (4th Edition ed.). London: Jones & Bartlett Learning.

World Databank. (2011, September 1). Health Nutrition and Population (HNP) Statistics. UAE, KSA, Qatar, Oman, Bahrain, and Kuwait.

World Health Organization. (2006). Medical Devices in Contemporary Health Care Systems and Services. *Regional Committee for the Eastern Mediterranean Fiftey-Third Session* (pp. 1-17). Isfahan: WHO Press.

World Health Organization. (2010). *Medical Devices: Managing the Mismatch: An Outcome of the Priority Medical Devices Project.* Geneva: WHO Press.

World Health Organization, WHO. (2011). *WHO Country Profile*. Retrieved September 1, 2011, from http://www.who.int/countries/qat/en/

Zain, A. A., & Shaaban, A. (2009, July 26). *Alternative medicine gaining ground in UAE*. Retrieved June 5, 2011, from Khaleej Times Online: http://www.khaleejtimes.com/displayarticlenew.asp?section=health&xfile=data/health/2009/july/health_july40.xml

Zawya. (2009, September 30). *GCC Healthcare Industry Set for Consistent Growth*. Retrieved August 31, 2011, from http://www.zawya.com/story.cfm/sidZAWYA20091001034616/GCC_healthcare_industry_set_for_consistent_growth?pass=1

Zawya. (2007, April 12). *GCC Takaful insurance growth to be exponential*. Retrieved Spetember 1, 2011, from http://www.zawya.com/story.cfm/sidZAWYA20070412074758/GCC_Takaful_insurance_growth_to_be_exponential

Zawya. (2011). *NCB: Saudi Healthcare Sector Report - 2011.* Abu Dhabi: National Commercial Bank NCB.

Zeithaml, V. A. (2009). *Delivering Quality Service.* New York: Simon and Schuster.

Further references:

Interview Transcription, Survey details and Case study can be found online under: http://www.gm.wiso.uni-erlangen.de/buecher/mes/

Schriften zur Gesundheitsökonomie

HERZ

Health Economics Research Zentrum
Buchweizenfeld 27
31303 Burgdorf
Fax: +49(0)5136/976187
email: herz@schoeffski.de

Bisher erschienen:

Band 1 *Steininger-Niederleitner, M., Sohn, S., Schöffski, O. (2003)*
Managed Care in der Schweiz und Übertragungsmöglichkeiten nach Deutschland
ISBN 3-936863-00-8, 172 S., 18 Abb., Geb. EUR 19,90

Band 2 *Esslinger, A. S. (2003)*
Qualitätsorientierte strategische Planung und Steuerung in einem sozialen Dienstleistungsunternehmen mit Hilfe der Balanced Scorecard
ISBN 3-936863-01-6, 276 S., 36 Abb., 50 Tab., Geb. EUR 29,90

Band 3 *Lindenthal, J., Sohn, S., Schöffski, O. (2004)*
Praxisnetze der nächsten Generation: Ziele, Mittelverteilung und Steuerungsmechanismen
ISBN 3-936863-02-4, 216 S., 16 Abb., 19 Tab., Geb. EUR 24,90

Band 4 *Steinbach, H., Sohn, S., Schöffski, O. (2004)*
Möglichkeiten der Kalkulation von sektorenübergreifenden Kopfpauschalen (Capitation)
ISBN 3-936863-03-2, 312 S., 22 Abb., 28 Tab., Geb. EUR 29,90

Band 5 *Glock, G., Sohn, S., Schöffski, O. (2004)*
IT-Unterstützung für den medizinischen Prozess in der integrierten Versorgung
ISBN 3-936863-04-0, 208 S., 22 Abb., Geb. EUR 24,90

Band 6 *Hagn, D., Schöffski, O. (2005)*
Orphan Drugs. A Challenge for the Pharmaceutical Industry in Europe
ISBN 3-936863-05-9, 160 S., 37 Abb., 20 Tab., Geb. EUR 19,90

Band 7 *Pelleter, J., Sohn, S., Schöffski, O. (2004)*
Medizinische Versorgungszentren. Grundlagen, Chancen und Risiken einer neuen Versorgungsform
ISBN 3-936863-06-7, 196 S., 18 Abb., Geb. EUR 24,90

Band 8 *Sohn, S. (2006)*
Integration und Effizienz im Gesundheitswesen. Instrumente und ihre Evidenz für die integrierte Versorgung
ISBN 3-936863-07-5, 288 S., 26 Abb., 28 Tab., Geb. EUR 29,90

Band 9 *Hämmerle, P., Estelmann, A., Schwandt, M., Schöffski, O. (2006)*
Moderne Verfahren der Qualitätsberichterstattung im Krankenhaus
ISBN 3-936863-08-3, 140 S., 33 Abb., Geb. EUR 19,90

Band 10 *Marschall, D. (2007)*
Positionierung einer erfolgreichen Arzneimittelmarke
ISBN 978-3-936863-09-3, 244 S., 54 Abb., 24 Tab., Geb. EUR 24,90

Band 11 *Haarländer, S., Bühner, A., Schwandt, M., Schöffski, O. (2007)*
Public Private Partnership (PPP) im Krankenhausbereich
ISBN 978-3-936863-10-9, 192 S., 32 Abb., 3 Tab., Geb. EUR 24,90

Band 12 *Schmitt-Rüth, S., Esslinger, A. S., Schöffski, O. (2007)*
Der Markt für Medizintechnik – Analyse der Entwicklungen im Wandel der Zeit
ISBN 978-3-936863-11-6, 172 S., 20 Abb., 6 Tab., Geb. EUR 19,90

Band 13 *Sauer, F. (2007)*
Erfolgsfaktoren für das marktorientierte Management patentgeschützter Arzneimittel
ISBN 978-3-936863-12-3, 388 S., 54 Abb., 29 Tab., Geb. EUR 34,90

Band 14 *Emmert, M. (2008)*
Pay for Performance (P4P) im Gesundheitswesen – Ein Ansatz zur Verbesserung der Gesundheitsversorgung?
ISBN 978-3-936863-12-3, 460 S., 41 Abb., 77 Tab., Geb. EUR 39,90

Band 15 *Patzak, M. (2009)*
Alternative Finanzierungsinstrumente für Krankenhäuser
ISBN 978-3-936863-14-7, 320 S., 340 Abb., 28 Tab., Geb. EUR 39,90

Band 16 *Heil, A., Schwandt, M., Schöffski, O. (2009)*
Darstellung ärztlicher Weiterbildungskosten im Krankenhaus
ISBN 978-3-936863-15-4, 156 S., 9 Abb., 8 Tab., Geb. EUR 24,90

Band 17 *Held, S., Bolte, C., Bierbaum, M., Schöffski, O. (2009)*
Impact of Big Pharma organizational structure on R&D productivity
ISBN 978-3-936863-16-1, 160 S., 22 Abb., 29 Tab., Geb. EUR 24,90

Band 18 *Lauerer, M., Emmert, M., Schöffski, O. (2011)*
Die Qualität des deutschen Gesundheitswesens im internationalen Vergleich
ISBN 978-3-936863-17-8, 204 S., 14 Abb., 27 Tab., Geb. EUR 24,90

Band 19 *Scheppach, M., Emmert, M., Schöffski, O. (2011)*
Pay for Performance (P4P) im Gesundheitswesen: Leitfaden für eine erfolgreiche Einführung
ISBN 978-3-936863-18-5, 184 S., 23 Abb., 18 Tab., Geb. EUR 24,90

Band 20 *Pelleter, J. (2012)*
Organisatorische und institutionelle Herausforderungen bei der Implementierung von Integrierten Versorgungskonzepten am Beispiel der Telemedizin
ISBN 978-3-936863-19-2, 675 S., 67 Abb., 10 Tab., Geb. EUR 49,90

Band 21 *Kloep, M. (2012)*
Managed Equipment Services as a Conceptual Business Opportunity Model for the GCC with Focus on UAE - An Institutional and Economic Analysis.
ISBN 978-3-936863-20-8, 212 S., 17 Abb., 22 Tab., Geb. EUR 24,90